Midwest Living®

GREAT LAKES GETAWAYS

ALL NEW

Meredith® Books
Des Moines, Iowa

The Great Lakes beguile summertime visitors with an irresistible combination of blue waters, bright skies and sandy shorelines. From backroads to big cities, we've chosen 16 sunny Great Lakes destinations for relaxing, just-right-for-you weekends or on-the-go weeklong adventures. You'll find lodging tips that include cozy bed and breakfasts, posh lakeside resorts and historic hotels. We tell you about mom-and-pop cafes where the soup-and-sandwich specials set you back less than $5 and about big-city food festivals where you can eat your way around the world. And, of course, we mention the must-see sights and attractions along the way.

In each chapter, a few pages give you detailed accounts about a town or two, then we move on to a travel planner that lists places to stay and to eat, annual events, nearby attractions you won't want to miss and phone numbers to call for more information. Each region includes a basic map and full-color photos that show off some of the people and places that make these Midwest destinations the special vacation spots they are.

Mackinac Island bicyclists, page 110.

LAKE SUPERIOR

You might mistake it for an ocean, this boundless body of water that straddles the U.S.-Canadian border. In fact, at 31,820 square miles, Lake Superior claims the title of the largest freshwater lake in the world. It crowns the Heartland, stretching 350 miles from Minnesota on the west, across northern Wisconsin and on to Michigan's Upper Peninsula (UP), where it defines the UP's northern limits. It's the deepest of the Great Lakes, plunging to a chilly, midnight-blue depth of 1,280 feet.

The land along Lake Superior provides surprising contrasts. More than a century of mining and timbering built the tireless port cities of Duluth, Minnesota; Superior, Wisconsin; and Sault Ste. Marie, Michigan. Here, world-circling freighters shoulder their way into harbors around the clock, filling their bellies with the riches of the Upper Midwest—grain, iron ore, coal and oil—then heading east to the shipping lanes of the St. Lawrence Seaway and the Atlantic Ocean beyond.

Away from the pockets of industry, Lake Superior's shoreline gives way to long stretches of sandy beaches and harbors bristling with the bobbing masts of pleasure boats. Lighthouses keep lonely vigils on rocky outcroppings and comfortable small towns nestle in sheltered bays. In some places the lake adjoins million-acre state and national parks—vast forested tracts that look much like the untamed wilderness that greeted the area's earliest settlers. Delicate wildflowers thrive in shaded woods and sunlit clearings; rivers run deep and clear. Hiking and biking trails lead to hidden waterfalls and overlooks that reveal lake vistas.

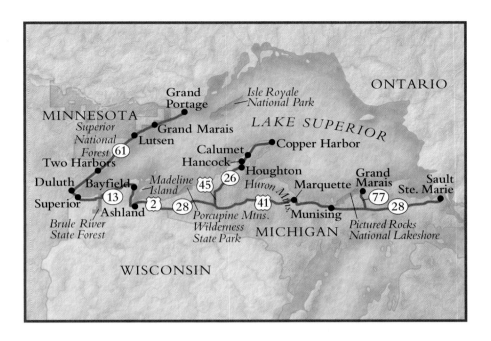

Head up Minnesota's Lake Superior "coast"—called the North Shore—and you'll discover a landscape of craggy cliffs, lighthouse-crowned ridges and rivers tumbling to the great lake. You can follow scenic State-61 for 150 miles, all the way to Canada, stopping along the way for local delicacies such as wild rice and smoked fish.

In Bayfield, Wisconsin (recently named Best Little Town in the Midwest by the *Chicago Tribune*), a gentle hillside decorated with Victorian houses steps down to a harbor ringed with small shops and restaurants. A ferry takes visitors to lovely Madeline Island, a 20-minute ride away.

On Michigan's Keweenaw Peninsula, glorious Victorian opera houses and ghostly mining towns recall a prosperous past, when the discovery of copper so pure it rivaled any in the world brought boom times.

Marquette, Michigan, is the town that iron built. Visitors come for the tasty pastry pockets called pasties, a meat-and-vegetable pie once favored by miners. They come, too, for a chance to take a picture of the town's bright red lighthouse, the most photographed along the Great Lakes.

MINNESOTA'S NORTH SHORE

Duluth's urban charms give way to an inviting wilderness landscape worth exploring.

Lake Superior meets Minnesota in a dramatic blending of land and water. The result is a landscape of craggy shorelines, high forest-crowned ridges and two dozen rivers that tumble down rocky gorges in their rush to the great lake. Dubbed the North Shore, Minnesota's Lake Superior "coast" extends 150 miles along the eastern edge of an arrowhead of land that juts out to form the state's northeast corner.

At its base thrives the port of Duluth, gateway to the North Shore; at the point stands Grand Portage, the last stop before Canada. In between are cozy harbor towns and log-cabin resorts where the hospitality remains as enduring as the lake and surrounding pines.

Surprising Duluth

I-35 whisks travelers along the short 156 miles from Minneapolis to Duluth. As the highway bends to reveal Duluth, you're likely to catch your breath in delight. Gabled homes step down leafy hills to a port busy with shipping and a glittering Lake Superior that stretches to the horizon.

Its spectacular natural harbor was the key to the city's 19th-century prosperity. Ships carried iron and lumber from the area that surrounded the lake to a waiting world. Today, Duluth is the Great Lakes' busiest port, nurturing a culturally and commercially vibrant town of 85,000 people.

Duluth's most prominent landmark is the Aerial Lift Bridge, a towering web of silvery steel girders that rises 138 feet in less than a minute as ships approach. Freighters flying flags from around the world pass beneath it. Leaning out from the bridge's adjoining promenade, you almost can touch their giant hulls as they glide by.

Stretching along the lakeshore for 17 miles and extending inland only 4 miles, Duluth pairs an appealing 19th-century facade with a lively, thoroughly modern lifestyle. Inside wind-worn brick storefronts along Lake Avenue north of Canal Park, shoppers browse for regional art, home decorations, books, toys and clothing. Across the

DULUTH CONVENTION & VISITORS BUREAU

Duluth's Central Administration Building is a century-old landmark.

Aerial Lift Bridge, Lake Avenue threads through Park Point, a 7-mile spit of land where summertime crowds flock to sandy beaches for swimming and sunbathing. In the evening, diners fill harborside restaurants and bars, and watch the city's night lights surf the harbor's gentle waves.

In Bayfront Festival Park, home to a year-round series of arts, music and sports festivals, children clamber over Playfront, a wood, fortresslike playground. Across I-35 stands the 1890s depot in its original Victorian-era splendor, now serving as a heritage-and-art center with four museums. Board the North Shore Scenic Railroad here for a 26-mile ride through aspen groves and across sheer-sided gorges to the turn-of-the-century depot at Two Harbors (population: 3,600), the next major community along the North Shore.

Up the Shore

Ore barons founded Two Harbors in 1884 as a port to ship out iron mined farther inland. Giant ore boats still dock in Two Harbors to take on loads of iron ore, then slip out under the watchful eye of the Lighthouse Point beacon. The red brick, white-trimmed lighthouse (open for tours) peers out over the vast lake to the south and the rising forests to the north.

You'll see the changing face of Lake Superior's shoreline while heading north on State-61. Cliffs standing high above the waves give way to rocky beaches, forests seem to wade into the surf, and rivers rush to empty their waters into the lake.

Near Castle Danger, 14 miles north of Two Harbors, the Gooseberry River cascades over two 30-foot waterfalls in Gooseberry Falls State Park. Near Silver Bay, 21 miles farther up the shore, the Baptism River plummets more than 80 feet in Tettegouche State Park. You'll discover several noteworthy Lake Superior landmarks between these two state parks.

The natural wonders include the cathedrallike buttresses of Shovel Point and Palisade Head's 200-foot-high cliffs. The Split Rock Lighthouse balances like an ocher-and-white chess pawn on a sheer rock outcropping. Crews who built the lighthouse in 1910 hoisted materials up the 170-foot

Bright sun and brisk breezes create easy sailing in Duluth.

DULUTH CONVENTION & VISITORS BUREAU

Hiking and biking trails wind through Grand Portage State Park.

LAYNE KENNEDY

cliff, using a rope and pulley. The lens guided ships past the treacherous shoreline until 1969. Today, you can tour the lightkeeper's restored home and climb the tower for unparalleled views of the North Shore.

Farther up the shore, State-61 skirts the 10,000 square miles of Superior National Forest. Its trees cover the bulk of this triangular land mass between Lake Superior and the Canadian border, interrupted occasionally by a bold, bald bluff that provides panoramas of wilderness. The mountains reach great heights at Lutsen, a ski resort with the highest downhill runs in the Midwest. In the summer, mountain bikers challenge the resort's slopes.

Grand Marais and Grand Portage

Three-fourths of the way up the North Shore is the one-time fishing village of Grand Marais (population: 1,100). It hugs a natural harbor of Lake Superior 18 miles up the shore and supports a thriving arts

community. Just steps from the lake, you can meander through the downtown of old cottages converted into craft shops and galleries.

Heading inland from Grand Marais, the Gunflint Trail (County-12) weaves through evergreens and past lakes to the Boundary Waters Canoe Area. Resorts along the Gunflint attract canoeists, kayakers and anglers in summer. Their groomed trails draw snowmobilers, cross-country skiers and mushers in winter.

At the North Shore's tip in Grand Portage (population: 250), 18th-century fur trappers rendezvoused for rest, merrymaking and trade. Little has changed. A reconstructed North West Company fur-trading post from the late 1700s provides a glimpse into the lives of the area's first European visitors. The Grand Portage Lodge and Casino offers today's visitors rest and revelry. At Grand Portage State Park, the Pigeon River roars over a 120-foot drop of rock ledges, the highest waterfall in the state, nature's final wonder along Minnesota's North Shore.

Planning Your Visit to the North Shore

For more information, contact: Minnesota Office of Tourism (800/657-3700).

AREA RECREATION

Biking—The Superior Mountain Bike Trail includes 130 miles of trails through Superior National Forest. Many resorts and lodges offer biking packages. Contact: Lutsen-Tofte Tourism Assoc. (218/663-7804 or 1-888/61-NORTH).

Hiking—The Superior Hiking Trail tracks State-61's route from Two Harbors to the Canadian border, with several trail heads along the way (218/834-2700). Sign up for lodge-to-lodge hikes with over-nights at local lodges and bed and breakfasts, sack breakfasts and lunches, and a luggage shuttle. Boundary Country Trekking (800/322-8327).

Kayaking—The Lake Superior Water Trail has campsites and stops along 19 miles of shoreline between Gooseberry Falls State Park near Castle Danger and Tettegouche State Park near Silver Bay (888/646-6367).

Excursions—The 115-foot, 150-passenger *Grampa Woo* cruises the North Shore and sails to Isle Royale. Depart from Two Harbors, Beaver Bay and Grand Marais (218/226-4100).

Scenic Drive—Four-lane State-61 hurries from Duluth to Two Harbors, but Old Highway-61 follows the shoreline through small communities. (Watch for shops selling smoked fish, a local favorite.) In fall, autumn color rolls through in waves: The maples flare orange then red along the slopes of the Sawtooth Mountains in September before the aspens and birches turn gold nearer the shore in October. Contact: North Shore Scenic Drive Assoc., Box 240, Knife River, MN 55609-0240.

Duluth

For information, contact: Duluth Convention & Visitors Bureau (800/4-DULUTH).

LODGINGS

Motels include the harborside Holiday Inn and Radisson. Other choices: Comfort Suites Canal—This classy harborside motel in Canal Park has a veranda that wraps around the building. Doubles from $109 (218/727-1378).

Fitger's Inn—Located in the historic Fitger's Brewery on the shore of Lake Superior, the Inn's 60 rooms and suites are decorated with Georgian-style furnishings. Doubles from $85 (800/726-2982).

The Mansion—This bed and breakfast offers 10 lavish rooms and a three-bedroom gardener's apartment in a shoreside manor. Doubles from $105 (218/724-0739).

DINING

Grandma's Saloon and Grill—This long-standing eatery in the shadows of the Aerial Lift Bridge has a menu full of specialties: thick, juicy burgers and steaks; Italian sandwiches and pasta; fresh Lake Superior fish; and homemade cheesecake (218/727-4192).

The Pickwick—An Old World air distinguishes this 1914 lakefront landmark known for walleye, grilled steaks and chops (218/727-8901).

SHOPPING

Duluth Pack Store—Buy canvas and leather goods from briefcases to coats. Ask for a catalog (218/722-1707).

ACTIVITIES

North Shore Scenic Railroad—Take short or daylong excursions along Lake Superior's shore to Two Harbors (800/423-1273).

Vista Fleet Harbor Cruises—Enjoy narrated tours and dinner cruises of the harbor (218/722-6218).

HISTORIC SITES

St. Louis County Heritage and Arts Center—An 1890s depot houses displays about railroading and area history, as well as a children's museum. (888/727-8025).

Glensheen—Architecture and design buffs praise the Arts and Crafts panache of this 39-room shorefront mansion (888/454-GLEN).

Lakewalk—From Canal Park beside the bridge, the Lakewalk curves along the shoreline northeast to the Rose

The steel webbing of Duluth's massive landmark, the Aerial Lift Bridge, frames a passing freighter.

Garden, where 3,000 bushes bloom in summer.

Marine Museum—Learn about the adventures and misadventures of commercial shipping. A U.S. Army Corps of Engineers museum is in Canal Park (218/727-2497).

The William A. Irvin—Tour a retired 610-foot ore freighter now docked as a floating museum. Once the flagship of U.S. Steel's Great Lakes Fleet, it boasts posh accommodations (218/722-7876).

FESTIVALS

Bayfront Blues Festival—In August, international blues artists and bands perform on two concert stages (715/394-6831).

Beargrease Sled Dog Marathon—This 500-mile round-trip race from Duluth to Grand Portage tests 30 mushing teams. Five-day race begins in mid-January (218/722-7631).

Grandma's Marathon—Two-decades-old June marathon winds along the North Shore. Spectators engage in other events such as all-you-can-eat spaghetti dinners and a health expo (800/4-DULUTH).

Two Harbors

Founded in 1884 to ship iron ore, Two Harbors once was crowded with freighters lining up to take on loads of taconite, then ship out under the watchful eye of the Lighthouse Point beacon. The town is a handy port of call for visitors exploring the North Shore. Contact: Two Harbors Chamber of Commerce (800/777-7384).

DINING

Russ Kendall's Smoked Fish House—On scenic Old Highway-61 just south of Knife River, sugar-smoked trout and salmon is ready to eat on site or take along (218/834-5995).

Scenic Cafe—Midway between Duluth and Two Harbors along the North Shore Scenic Drive, this eatery boasts imaginative vegetarian dishes, luscious desserts and an extensive beer and wine list (218/525-6274).

SHOPPING

Silver Creek Pioneer Crafts—Located northeast of Two Harbors along State-61, this shop carries only handmade crafts, artwork and postcards by local artists (218/834-4995).

AREA ATTRACTIONS

Depot Museum—This 1907 attraction spotlights the area's mining heritage (218/834-4898).

TRAVEL GUIDE

Gooseberry Falls State Park—Enjoy waterfall views and scenic overlooks 13 miles northeast of Two Harbors. The visitors center houses exhibits about North Shore history (218/834-3855). Lighthouse Point and Harbor Museum—The old red brick lighthouse is now a museum devoted to iron ore shipping history (218/834-4898). Split Rock Lighthouse Historic Site—Perched high on a shoreline cliff 20 miles northeast of Two Harbors, from 1910 to 1969 this light warned ships away from rock-strewn shallows. Now, it's a museum with exhibits about Great Lakes shipping and lighthouse lore (218/226-6372). Snowmobiling—A vast network of trails leads snowmobilers through the wilderness. Contact: North Shore State Trail (218/834-6626).

Lutsen

The population of this town 94 miles northeast of Duluth swells each summer from two dozen permanent residents to 60,000. Visitors come to bike and hike the mountains surrounding the tiny hamlet. The area also is Minnesota's leading ski resort. Contact: Lutsen-

Tofte Tourism Assoc. (1-888/61-NORTH).

LODGINGS

Village Inn & Resort at Lutsen Mountains—Lodge rooms, condominiums and luxury homes offer views of Moose Mountain. Spas, pools and championship golf are also available. Doubles from $49 (800/642-6036). Bluefin Bay on Lake Superior—The lake is

outside the back doors of these two-story townhomes with full kitchens, fireplaces and whirlpool baths. From $139 (800/258-3346). Lutsen Resort— Minnesota's oldest resort includes a hand-carved timber lodge, cozy rooms, townhomes and log homes, plus a 9-hole golf course and 3 miles

of Lake Superior shoreline. Doubles from $75 (800/258-8736). Lindgren's Bed & Breakfast on Lake Superior—Hearty breakfasts are served fireside and lakeside in this 1920s rustic log home. Doubles from $85 (218/663-7450).

SHOPPING

The Kah-Nee-Tah Gallery— Look for paintings, pottery, stained glass,

Whatever the weather, there's a cozy fireside spot for family fun at the Village Inn & Resort in Lutsen.

LAYNE KENNEDY

baskets and carved wood by Minnesota artists 9 miles northeast of Lutsen along State-61 (800/216-2585).

ACTIVITIES

Alpine Slide—Eagle Mountain and Moose Mountain are part of the Lutsen Mountains. Ride a chairlift to the summit of Eagle Mountain and take a twisting half-mile slide back down (218/663-7281).

Sky Ride—The Gondola Skyride carries hikers and bikers on a mile-long, 10-minute ride to the top of Moose Mountain, where 100-mile views and a deli and restaurant await (218/663-7281).

WINTER ACTIVITIES

Cross-Country Skiing—North Shore Ski Trail includes 196 km of groomed trails from Schroeder to Grand Marais, with many lodges and outfitters providing equipment and maps (1-888/61-NORTH).

Lutsen Mountain Skiing—Plunge down one of 62 runs at Minnesota's oldest ski area (218/663-7281).

Grand Marais

Scandinavians founded this fishing port 110 miles northeast of Duluth. The harbor remains active with charter fishing and pleasure boats. The town is an artists' enclave. Contact: Grand Marais Chamber of Commerce (218/387-1400).

LODGINGS

Several motels overlook Lake Superior and national chains have properties in Grand Marais. Other options:

Naniboujou Lodge—Tucked beside the lake

15 miles northeast of Grand Marais and known for its Cree-inspired designs, this 1920s vintage lodge has garnered national attention. Doubles from $69 (218/387-2688).

Pincushion Mountain Bed and Breakfast—This secluded ridge-top retreat offers a sauna and dramatic lake views. Doubles from $90 (800/542-1226).

DINING

Angry Trout Cafe—Dine on char-grilled lake trout while gazing out at the harbor (218/387-1265).

Birch Terrace—This 50-year-old log mansion serves seafood and steaks (218/387-2215).

Blue Water Cafe—Relish homemade pies and crispy fries harborside (218/387-1597).

Loafer Bakery & Deli—Specialties include sandwiches on made-from-scratch rolls and huge chocolate chip cookies (218/387-1747).

SHOPPING

Sivertson Gallery—Lakeshore cottage sells works of local, Canadian and Alaskan artists (218/387-2491).

Viking Hus—Along State-61, this shop showcases Scandinavian wares (218/387-2589).

ACTIVITIES

Gunflint Trail—The old logging road (County-12)

runs from Grand Marais to the Boundary Waters Canoe Area Wilderness, with 27 resorts offering rooms, cabins and outfitters year-round. Contact: Gunflint Trail Assoc. (800/338-6932).

WINTER ACTIVITIES

Sleigh Rides at Okontoe—Twenty-seven miles up the Gunflint Trail, ride through the woods along Bow and Quiver lakes in a lantern-lit, horse-drawn sleigh (218/388-9423).

Grand Portage

Grand Portage (150 miles northeast of Duluth) nudges the Canadian border on Minnesota's northeastern tip.

LODGINGS

Grand Portage Lodge and Casino—This 100-room lodge overlooks the bay and has a lakeside restaurant. Doubles from $57 (800/543-1384).

ATTRACTIONS

Grand Portage State Park—The Pigeon River rushes over a 120-foot drop of rock ledges, Minnesota's highest waterfall (218/475-2360).

Grand Portage National Monument—Costumed guides enliven this reconstructed 1700s North West Company fur-trading post (218/387-2788).

By Eric Minton

THE BAYFIELD PENINSULA

A cluster of islands crowns northwestern Wisconsin's vacation playground.

Nature flexed its muscles in Wisconsin's northwestern corner. It's a land of towering pine forests where swift-running rivers tumble over steep precipices to create thunderous waterfalls. Along the region's northern edge, imposing sandstone bluffs and plucky shoreside villages brave the wild blue horizon of powerful Lake Superior.

Nature smiled here, too. The chilly rivers teem with trout, and along the Lake Superior shoreline, the Apostle Islands scatter across a broad bay—22 forested jewels gleaming like emeralds in the brilliant cobalt waters.

Since the days of the French voyageurs, ports here have shaped the state's history. Scalloped with coves and inlets, the shoreline that Wisconsin shares with Lake Superior forms fine natural harbors for mariners.

Still-grand buildings in Ashland, a small port city of 8,700 along Lake Superior's Chequamegon Bay, stand as reminders of the 19th-century wealth iron mining, logging and commercial fishing brought to these north-woods outposts. In Superior, 1,000-foot freighters haul coal, grain and iron ore across Lake Superior for shipment across America. Paired with its neighbor, Duluth, Minnesota, Superior rates as one of the busiest ports along all the Great Lakes.

Welcome Ashore

Away from the industrious port cities, the purely pleasurable qualities of Lake Superior reign. Fresh breezes roll off the lake and across the Bayfield Peninsula, a gently rounded land mass that noses into the lake between Ashland and Superior. With plenty of protected anchorages and deep, clear waters, the peninsula and the Apostle Islands arrayed at its tip are a seafarer's dream.

Vacationing boaters delight in puttering from town to town or island to island, with no greater ambition than a shore lunch. You can glide into the marina at Washburn, where clanging masts line up like church steeples, then stretch your legs along the lakeshore walking trail. Here, you'll find galleries filled with weavings and pottery by local artisans. The local charter fishing fleets ply waters renowned for their bountiful salmon, lake trout and whitefish.

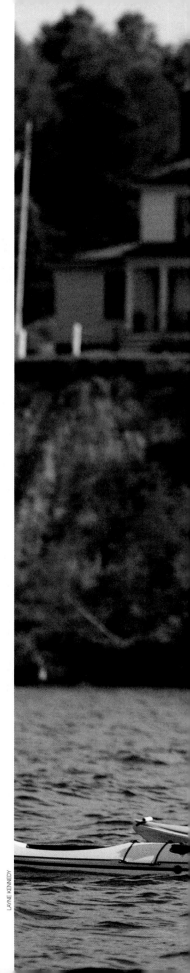

LAYNE KENNEDY

Kayaks pass a turn-of-the-century Apostle Islands lighthouse.

Boaters looking for an excursion can round the north end of the peninsula and head to tiny Cornucopia (population: 100), Wisconsin's northernmost community. Screeching seagulls reel above a broad ribbon of golden beach, and shopkeepers operate a handful of quaint shops, surprising in this sleepy little village.

Bayfield

The town of Bayfield anchors the region for mariners and non-mariners alike. This unspoiled community of about 700 residents charms visitors with its tree-lined streets, small shops and majestic old Victorian homes that sit high on the hill like watchful grandmothers overseeing the waterfront activities.

Artists and artisans who have found their way to this tranquil spot display their paintings, sculpture, weavings, carvings and glasswork in galleries scattered in and near town. At Eckels Pottery, visitors to northern Wisconsin's oldest working studio can see clay transformed into chunky flower pots and delicate tableware.

Performing artists like Bayfield, too. Just outside town is the Lake Superior Big Top Chautauqua. This 750-seat tent theater draws enthusiastic crowds to jazz, rock and country concerts, as well as original historic musicals.

The lake gentles the peninsula's weather, creating a long growing season that produces lush berries and flourishing fruit trees. On the first full weekend in October, bushels of apples crowd roadside stands, and the aroma of cinnamon-scented pies is in the air as 50,000 people trek to Bayfield for fun at the annual Apple Festival.

Near Bayfield's commercial port, snub-nosed fishing boats unload fresh whitefish for the local restaurants, where the sweet and subtle fish nearly always tops the menu as nightly specials.

Island Hopping

From almost anywhere in town, you're rewarded with stunning views of the Apostle Islands, which begin right offshore, seemingly close enough to touch. For an introduction to the national lakeshore, stop by the National Park Service Visitors Center in Bayfield. It's housed in the grand old county courthouse building, constructed of rich brownstone. (In the 1800s, brownstone was the material of choice for elegant buildings all over the Midwest.) Much of it was quarried here, on Basswood, Stockton and Hermit islands. At the visitors center,

The staff at Bayfield's Old Rittenhouse Inn.

PETER LINDMAN

16

La Pointe village on picturesque Madeline Island.

LAYNE KENNEDY

you can view an introduction to the islands, get maps and learn about ranger-led activities that include guided beach walks, campfire programs, and fish camp and lighthouse tours.

According to folklore, early explorers, counting just 12 islands, named this archipelago the Apostles. In truth, there are 22 islands; all but Madeline are part of the national lakeshore. Six lighthouses dot the islands, and most, including those on Sand and Raspberry islands, welcome summer visitors.

Oak and Stockton islands have well-worn hiking trails; Sand and Raspberry are popular for their beaches and bays. Swimming is for the hardy only—except in shallow bays, the water temperature rarely climbs above the 50s. But the lake here is blissfully clear. Most islands have designated campsites for tent camping.

For those without their own boats, Bayfield offers plenty of options for reaching the islands. Excursion boats depart daily in the summer months, winding through the islands, past light-houses and dramatic rock formations. Crew members share information about the area's history and natural resources. Marinas in town charter sailboats with or without captains. Water taxis deposit campers on the island of their choice—

and pick them up again.

Sea kayaks are perhaps the finest way to explore the islands. Low-slung and nimble, they can poke in and out of tight passages and the hollow maws of caves. Experienced paddlers head for Devil's Island and other islands at the north end of the national lakeshore, wave-torn and pockmarked from exposure to open seas. Even rank beginners can take to the waters on guided trips with local outfitters.

Ferries regularly make the short passage to Madeline Island, a 20-minute trip from Bayfield. You can bring a car, but you may prefer to rent a bike or moped to explore this 14-mile-long island. A popular vacation spot, Madeline boasts a full-service resort, a Robert Trent Jones-designed golf course, a marina and a state park. The ferry docks at La Pointe, the island's only town, where the Madeline Island Historical Museum recounts its early days as a fur trading post.

On the eastern shore, Big Bay State Park draws swimmers, birdwatchers and campers. Here, dawn often puts on a spectacular show, bathing the sky in peaches and pinks, before the sun shines brightly on another Apostle Islands summer day.

Planning Your Visit to the Bayfield Area

For more information, contact: Bayfield Chamber of Commerce (800/447-4094); Madeline Island Chamber of Commerce (888/475-3386); Ashland Area Chamber of Commerce (800/284-9484); Apostle Islands National Lakeshore (715/779-3397).

LODGINGS

You'll find several small motels in the Ashland and Bayfield area; book in advance for summer months. Others to try: Old Rittenhouse Inn— The queen of Bayfield's bed and breakfasts, the venerable Rittenhouse welcomes guests with its fabulous wraparound porch, wood-burning fireplaces, antique furnishings, whirlpools and gourmet dining. Doubles from $119 (715/779-5111). Cooper Hill House— Situated on a hill above Bayfield's ferry dock, this 1888 home is a casual bed and breakfast. Each room has a private bath. Doubles from $79 (715/779-5060). Bodin's Bayfield Resort— Cottages overlook Lake Superior in Bayfield. Spacious grounds and a sand beach enhance the setting. Doubles from $65 (715/373-2359). Hotel Chequamegon— Since the late 1800s, this grand hotel has graced the shores of Lake Superior in Ashland. Twice risen from the ashes, it was completely rebuilt in 1986. You'll find rich decor and attentive service. Doubles from $85 (800/946-5555). The Inn on Madeline Island—This full-service, family-friendly resort along the water offers condominiums, cottages, swimming pool, beach, tennis courts and more. Doubles from $89 (800/822-6315). Thimbleberry Inn—With 375 feet of Lake Superior frontage, this home includes three guest rooms, each with a private entrance, private bath and fireplace. Half-day and full-day sailing trips are available on the owner's 35-foot wooden ketch. Doubles from $75, with full breakfast (715/779-5757). Dreamcatcher—Overlooking Lake Superior, this five-room lodge (private baths and entrances) and two cottages share extensive grounds and a sauna. It's within walking distance of downtown Bayfield. Doubles from $62 (715/779-5538). Silvernail Guest House— This 19th-century home has been renovated with private baths, double whirlpools and antiques. Doubles from $85 (715/779-5575). Winfield Inn—Motel-style units and kitchenette apartments on Lake Superior provide great views of the Apostle Islands. Doubles from $35 (715/779-3252).

CAMPING

Apostle Islands National Lakeshore—Camp at designated sites and in the back country on 18 of the islands. Permits required; fee. (715/779-3397). Big Bay—Big Bay State Park has 51 rustic sites on Madeline Island's sandy Big Bay (715/779-4020). Adjacent to the state park, the town of La Pointe operates a campground with 44 rustic sites on a first-come, first-served basis. Chequamegon National Forest—This immense 860,000-acre forest begins west of Washburn and stretches south, with 24 campgrounds. Contact: Chequamegon National Forest (715/762-2461). Dalrymple Campground— Rustic tent and RV sites overlook Lake Superior just north of Bayfield (715/779-5712). Little Sand Bay—This private campground has 23 sites, hookups, a beach and boat ramp (715/779-5235 or 715/779-7007).

DINING

The Clubhouse—This hot spot on Madeline gets better every year, with

California-style cuisine that features inventive game-bird dishes and homestyle fare with a twist such as horseradish mashed potatoes. There's a top-notch wine list, too. Reservations recommended (715/747-2612). The Pub—Enjoy

the eclectic decor at this popular Bayfield spot for casual fare (715/779-5641). Old Rittenhouse Inn—Splurge with a fixed-price dinner menu that includes seasonal fruit soups and trout au champagne. About $100 for dinner for two

and barbecue ribs top the menu at this water-front spot overlooking the Washburn marina (715/373-5492). The Depot—The 1888 train depot in Ashland features fine dining with a Friday fish fry and fresh whitefish specials (715/682-4200).

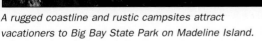
A rugged coastline and rustic campsites attract vacationers to Big Bay State Park on Madeline Island.

SIGHTSEEING

Lake Superior Big Top Chautauqua—Dubbed the "Carnegie Hall of Tent Shows," this canvas tent theater 3 miles south of Bayfield hosts concerts, variety shows and original historical musicals such as *Riding the Wind*, celebrating life in the Apostle Islands (888/244-8368). Ashland History—The 23-room Wilmarth Mansion, built in 1869, welcomes visitors in its present-day role as the Ashland Museum. For an informal walking tour of downtown Ashland's historic lumber-era buildings, stop by the Ashland Area Chamber of Commerce, 320 Fourth Ave. W., (800/284-9484).

sandwiches and fresh fish in a casual eatery overlooking Lake Superior on Madeline Island. Be sure to ask for a seat on the comfortable screened porch (800/822-6315). Maggie's—Pink flamingos are just the beginning of

(715/779-5111). Village Inn—Try the supper club-style fare in Cornucopia. Ask about whitefish livers as an appetizer— they're a local specialty (715/742-3941). The Steak Pit—Char-broiled steaks, prime rib

OUTDOOR ADVENTURES

Apostle Islands National Lakeshore—The park service can direct you to hiking trails, beaches, lighthouses, historic spots of interest and more. Don't overlook the mainland portions of the park, with attractions such as the Hokenson Brothers Fishery, a restored commercial fishing operation at Little Sand Bay (715/779-3397). Boat Charters—Choose from several sportfishing charters and bareboat or crewed sailboat charters in the Bayfield area. For a list of charter operations, contact: Bayfield Chamber of Commerce (800/447-4094). Kayaking—Trek & Trail in Bayfield offers sea kayak rentals, lessons and half-day to weeklong trips to the islands (800/354-8735). Boat Cruises—Apostle Island Cruise service provides a variety of narrated trips to view lighthouses, sea caves and shipwrecks May through October (800/323-7619). Schooner Sailing—Sail the Apostles aboard *Zeeto*, a 54-foot three-masted schooner. Sailing adventures (3½-hours) depart mornings, afternoons and evenings June through September. Apostle Islands Cruise Service (800/323-7619). Prentice Park—Ashland's largest city park features nature walks along Fish Creek Slough, a fine spot to see migrating birds and waterfowl (800/284-9484). Madeline Island Ferry—

Sailboats explore the shorelines of the 22 isles that make up the Apostle Islands National Lakeshore.

There are several departures daily. Passengers, bikes and vehicles are permitted. Bus tours of Madeline Island are available in season (715/747-2051). Mountain Biking—Some of Wisconsin's finest mountain biking trails lie about 25 miles southwest of Ashland in the Hayward/Cable area and adjacent Chequamegon National Forest. For maps and trail information, contact: Cable Area Chamber of Commerce (800/533-7454) or Chequamegon National Forest (715/762-2461).

FESTIVALS

The Red Cliff Indian Reservation treats visitors to the Red Cliff Traditional Pow-Wow in early July (715/779-5437). Sailboats scoot across the local waters in a series of regattas during Bayfield Race Week in late June or early July (800/447-4094). Wooden boats of all shapes and sizes take over during the Wooden Boat Rendezvous in mid-August (800/447-4094).

Sample homemade apple pies at Bayfield's Apple Festival the first week in October (800/447-4094).

WINTER ACTIVITIES

On the mainland portions of the national lakeshore, cross-country skiers and snowshoers explore the snow and ice formations that cling to the cliffs (715/779-3397). Skiers head for Mt. Ashwabay near Bayfield, with 13 downhill runs and 40 km of cross-country trails (715/779-3227).

OTHER PLACES TO VISIT

Amnicon Falls State Park—As the name suggests, a series of falls highlights this park, located 10 miles east of Superior. The Amnicon River tumbles over three waterfalls, each about 30 feet high, on its way to Lake Superior. A covered footbridge leads to an island with a view of the falls and rocky river gorge. Camping is available at 36 sites (715/399-3111).

Pattison State Park—This park, 10 miles south of Superior, preserves Wisconsin's highest waterfall, where the Black River plummets 165 feet. In fact, it's the fourth largest falls east of the Rockies. Hike below the falls on a trail that skirts the gorge, dramatic dark cliffs of basalt that gave the river its name. Camping is available (715/399-3111).

Duluth/Superior—These twin port towns make the lake accessible with charter fishing, tours of historic ships and more. Harbor cruises take passengers past the bustling docks, home to the world's largest grain elevators and iron-ore docks. Contact: Superior/Douglas County Tourist Information Center (800/942-5313).

Brule River State Forest—Known as "the river of presidents," it has attracted five of them, from Teddy Roosevelt to Dwight Eisenhower, to fish its trout waters. Brule River State Forest straddles the Bois Brule River for more than 30 miles, all the way to its mouth on Lake Superior east of the city of Superior. Whitewater paddlers favor the lower stretch, where the Brule squeezes through a narrow valley and drops an average of 17 feet per mile. The 40,000-acre forest offers camping, hiking and cross-country skiing (715/372-4866).

By Tina Lassen

LAYNE KENNEDY

Wisconsin enjoys a national reputation for its extensive and well-maintained system of biking trails.

THE KEWEENAW PENINSULA

Bright vacation pleasures await visitors to the rugged paradise known as Copper Country.

Blanketed with thick stands of white pine and rooted in rich veins of copper, the Keweenaw Peninsula was a vast storehouse of riches in the mid–1800s. For decades, it screamed with sawmills and roared with mining furnaces, spawning millionaires and boomtowns in remote outposts deep in the Michigan north woods.

The wealth of minerals and big lumber may be largely gone, but the rugged Keweenaw Peninsula's treasured beauty remains. Fanning northeast like a dorsal fin off the back of Michigan's Upper Peninsula, it includes craggy bluffs, hidden waterfalls, rolling white pine forests and deep, blue bays melting into the vastness of Lake Superior.

Houghton and Hancock

The twin towns of Houghton (population: 7,498) and Hancock (population: 4,547) serve as unofficial gateways to the Keweenaw. They face each other across Portage Lake, with homes and churches and unnervingly steep streets tumbling down the 500-foot bluffs. Below, the Portage Lift Bridge rises like an elevator to allow boats to pass. Watch for the bright blue passenger ferry, *Ranger III*, heading out on its 6-hour trip to remote Isle Royale National Park.

The 45-mile-long wilderness island rises out of Lake Superior between Michigan's Upper Peninsula and northeast Minnesota. No cars are permitted, but visitors see moose, foxes and even an occasional wolf in a pristine natural setting along miles of hiking trails.

Houghton is home to Michigan Technological University and its excellent Seaman Mineral Museum. You can view many of the museum's 30,000 specimens tracing the region's geological history. Hancock, too, claims a college: Suomi College, the only such Finnish–American institution in the nation. The Keweenaw boasts a rich Finnish heritage. You'll see it in the bilingual street signs in downtown Hancock and in the numbers of Finnish saunas throughout the peninsula.

Just north of Hancock, the mammoth shaft house of the Quincy Mine dominates the skyline. One of the richest copper mines ever discovered, it contains

TRAVEL, MICHIGAN

A six-hour ferry ride will take you to Isle Royale.

the world's largest steam hoist. Take an underground tour of the mine, venturing 2,000 feet into a hillside. Quincy Mine represents a key attraction of the new Keweenaw National Historical Park, which preserves the area's rich copper mining legacy and includes "cooperating sites" throughout the peninsula.

More Copper Country Towns

Eleven miles north is Calumet (population: 818). The region's copper boom centered around this community, where 47,000 people once lived. The fabulous wealth the boom generated remains evident today. Visitors marvel at the copper barons' opulent homes. They also admire the elegant sandstone and copper opera house, so grand that 19th-century greats Enrico Caruso and Sarah Bernhardt traveled by train from the East to perform here. (It's been restored as The Calumet Theatre, so check for a schedule of events and enjoy a performance in posh surroundings.)

Downtown streets boast fancy brick storefronts, many now being restored. You can follow a self-guided walking tour. Also make time for a stop at Coppertown USA Mining Museum. Kids love the hands-on exhibits—a fun way to learn about the copper boom.

Continue north to Eagle Harbor, a well-protected inlet offering welcome refuge for mariners on Lake Superior. In town, stop to visit the wonderfully creaky Eagle Harbor Store. Nearby, at the 1871 Eagle Harbor lighthouse, linger in museum buildings that trace the area's fishing, mining and shipping.

From Eagle Harbor, follow the signs to Brockway Mountain Drive. Dubbed "the most beautiful road in Michigan," it traces the spine of a high ridge to Copper Harbor. At a parking area midway, you can stop and appreciate the panorama of Lake Superior and the rolling forests of the Keweenaw.

Near the Keweenaw's northernmost point lies Copper Harbor, a town sparked by the copper rush. Fearing conflicts between the miners and local Indian tribes, the federal government constructed the stockaded Fort Wilkins in 1844. The fights never materialized, and the fort proved of little use.

Today, Fort Wilkins is part of an engaging state park wedged between Lake Superior and Lake Fanny Hooe. Several restored buildings within the fort's stockade are open for casual wandering, with costumed interpreters depicting life on the rugged frontier.

A smattering of restaurants, lodgings and shops spill across Copper Harbor, a

Copper Harbor's
Fort Wilkins
dates to 1844.

TRAVEL MICHIGAN

JOHN STRAUSS

Brockway Mountain Drive, Keweenaw Peninsula.

town surrounded by natural beauty. Near the state marina on the south end of Copper Harbor, several beaches are strewn with pretty agates along their shorelines.

Just a few miles south of town, the Estivant Pines Sanctuary preserves a virgin tract of white pines that were threatened by loggers' saws as recently as 1970. Follow signs off US-41 in downtown Copper Harbor. The adventurous should plan to hike or mountain-bike around the tip of the peninsula, a large swath of forest interrupted only by old logging roads and footpaths. Locals can direct you to wonderful Lake Superior bays and beaches.

Ghost Towns and Farmsteads

From Copper Harbor, US-41 slaloms through birches and maples as it winds southwest to Delaware. A bonafide ghost town with abandoned houses and deserted dirt streets, Delaware once thrived, thanks to a lucrative copper mine that removed more than 8 million pounds of copper in the mid-1800s. You

still can tour the first level of the mine, exploring on your own or with a guided tour.

Farther south near Chassell, waterfowl flock to the Sturgeon River Sloughs Natural Area, an immense wetlands of waving grasses and flat terrain not usually associated with the Keweenaw. Near a raised observation deck, a chipped-bark footpath traces the tops of the dikes, an excellent spot for birdwatching. Sandhill cranes, great blue herons and a variety of ducks frequent the Keweenaw each summer.

Near Keweenaw Bay, the Hanka Homestead is a step back in time: an unaltered Finnish farmstead that was established near the turn of the century. Follow a remote country road to a farmhouse and outbuildings built in the traditional Scandinavian log construction. Tours explain the hardworking Hanka family's daily life: growing food, smoking fish and caring for farm animals. The farm represents what many immigrant copper miners worked for—land of their own to farm in the beautiful countryside where they had labored underground.

Planning Your Visit to the Keweenaw Peninsula

For more information, contact: Keweenaw Tourism Council (800/338-7982); Upper Peninsula Travel & Recreation Assoc. (800/562-7134). Places listed here may be open only during the summer season. Please call.

LODGINGS

Chain motels are available in the Houghton/Hancock area. Elsewhere, mom-and-pop style motels and small bed and breakfasts prevail. Lake Breeze—An old-fashioned lodge with a large porch nestles along Lake Superior in Eagle Harbor. The simple rooms have private baths. Doubles from $55 (906/289-4514). Laurium Manor Inn—Live the life of a copper baron in this opulent mansion near Calumet in Laurium. Among the highlights are elephant-hide wall-coverings, hand-carved fireplaces and silver-leaf ceiling detailing. Doubles from $49 (906/337-2549). Keweenaw Mountain Lodge—This rustic 1930s pine lodge near Copper Harbor offers motel-style rooms and one- to three-bedroom cabins. There's a golf course on the property.

Doubles from $65 (906/289-4403). Norland Motel—Stay in simple, clean rooms in Copper Harbor on the northwest shore of lovely Lake Fanny Hooe. Some offer kitchenettes and decks. Doubles from $44 (906/289-4815). Sand Hills Lighthouse Inn—Perched on a point on the Keweenaw Peninsula's northern shore, guests at this 1917 lighthouse enjoy 3,000 feet of Lake Superior shoreline. You can climb the tower, too. Eight Victorian-style rooms have private baths; some have private balconies. Doubles from $125, including full breakfast (906/337-1744). Belknap's Garnet House—Copper money built this turn-of-the-century mansion in Kearsage, originally owned by the manager of a nearby mine. The house includes five bedrooms (three with private baths) in a wooded setting. Doubles from $60 (906/337-5607).

CAMPING

Lake Fanny Hooe Resort—The south end of Lake Fanny Hooe is a good location for RVs in Copper Harbor. A club room, shower room, laundromat, beach, canoes and paddleboats are on site. Motel-style rooms are available

(800/426-4451). Fort Wilkins State Park—Camp at two excellent campgrounds with 165 modern sites, many right on the shore of Lake Fanny Hooe; some have hookups. See Outdoor Adventures on page 28 for more information. Reservations are recommended in July and August (800/44-PARKS). F. J. McLain State Park—Modern campsites dot the shore of Lake Superior near Hancock. All 103 sites have hookups. Rustic cabins are available. See Outdoor Adventures on page 28 for more information. Reservations are recommended (800/44-PARKS). Hancock Recreational Boating & Camping Facility—This location along the Portage canal in Hancock has 52 RV sites with hookups and 15 secluded tent sites (906/482-2720).

DINING

Kaleva Cafe—A friendly locals' spot, this diner-style eatery in Hancock is a great place to try the miner's pasty (a pot-pie-style blend of beef, potatoes, rutabagas and onion)—a specialty of the Upper Peninsula (906/482-1230). Harbor Haus—The waitresses perform the can-can for ferry passengers when the

Isle Royale Queen III passes by this bustling lakefront restaurant in Copper Harbor. It is known for German specialties such as sauerbraten and Wiener schnitzel; serves excellent whitefish, too (906/289-4502).

Toni's Country Kitchen— Famous for its immense pasties, this spot also offers unique and delicious Finnish baked goods (906/337-0611).

The Pines—A crackling fireplace and homemade

Mariner's Inn— This Copper Harbor institution lost some of its spirit when the original log building burned to the ground a few years ago, but it has regained its popularity as a gathering place for steaks and seafood. Try the salad bar and Friday fish-fry buffet, too (906/289-4637).

Shoreline Restaurant— Homemade pies are the biggest draw at this Eagle Harbor eatery, but

looking the lift bridge and the town of Houghton (906/482-8494).

Lindell's Chocolate Shop—Stop for a treat in Lake Linden, where Lindell's Chocolate Shop has been serving homemade ice cream and other goodies to patrons in gleaming old wooden booths since the 1920s (906/296-0793).

Onigaming Supper Club—South of Houghton, this classic northwoods supper club with a knotty pine dining room provides views of Portage Lake. Fresh fish specials top the menu (906/482-2714).

SIGHTSEEING

Seaman Mineral Museum—Michigan's official mineral museum is located on the fifth floor of the Electrical Energy Resources Center on the Michigan Technological University campus in Houghton. Open Mondays through Fridays all year, as well as Saturdays in summer (906/487-2572).

Keweenaw National Historical Park—One of the nation's newest national parks, the Keweenaw National Historical Park was established in 1992 to commemorate the heritage of copper mining on the Keweenaw Peninsula. Rather than preserving one tract of land, the park includes

JOHN STRAUSS

The copper mines were thriving when Belknap's Garnet House was built in Kearsage at the turn of the century.

cinnamon rolls make this tiny cafe in downtown Copper Harbor a great spot for rainy-day breakfasts. Delicious soups, sandwiches and local fish specialties keep folks coming all day (906/289-4222).

there's plenty of other home-style cooking featured on the menu (906/289-4441).

Portage Landing— Located at the Ramada Inn in Hancock, this restaurant features reliably good cooking and a great location over-

TRAVEL GUIDE

sites located throughout the peninsula, including the Calumet Historic District, the Quincy Mine Hoist, the Delaware Copper Mine and the Keweenaw County Historical Museum. Contact: Keweenaw Tourism Council (800/338-7982).
Hanka Homestead— Many Scandinavian immigrants traveled to the Keweenaw to work in the copper mines, saving their money to establish a self-sufficient life farming. The Hanka Homestead near Baraga preserves a Finnish homestead from the turn of the century. Call for hours (906/334-2601).

OUTDOOR ADVENTURES
Fort Wilkins State Park—This well-preserved example of a 19th-century military post lets visitors explore the routines of the military assigned to this remote 1844 outpost. The park has some short hiking trails along the shores of Lake Superior and Lake Fanny Hooe. Boat tours are offered to the Copper Harbor Lighthouse. Contact: Fort Wilkins State Park, Copper Harbor (906/289-4215; for reservations: 800/44-PARKS).
F. J. McLain State Park—Lake Superior is the top draw at this state park 8 miles north of Hancock. The park

boasts a campground, swimming beach and spectacular sunsets. Hike the 3-mile loop past Bear Lake or follow the 2-mile fitness trail. (906/482-0278).
Estivant Pines Sanctuary—Local conservationists saved this 377-acre tract of old-growth white pines by raising money to purchase the land and create the Estivant Pines Sanctuary. Now, you can take a walk among these towering trees, a world that feels almost primordial. Turn south off US-41 in Copper Harbor at the marked signs for Lake Manganese and Estivant Pines. Travel 2.3 miles down a backwoods dirt road, then turn right on Burma Road, traveling another .6 miles to the parking area.
Keweenaw Adventure Company—This local outfitter in Copper Harbor offers explorations of the Keweenaw in a variety of energetic ways, with mountain bike rentals, kayaking lessons and dogsledding classes (906/289-4303).
Waterfalls—A dozen impressive waterfalls cascade in the backcountry of the Keweenaw. Some are within easy walks of roads; others require more substantial hikes. For directions to some of

the finest, ask for the "Keweenaw Waterfalls" brochure. Contact: Keweenaw Tourism Council (800/338-7982).
Isle Royale Line—The ferry that carries hikers and lodgers out to Isle Royale National Park, the *Isle Royale Queen III*, also does casual duty on summer evenings, with 2½-hour sunset cruises out of Copper Harbor. You'll pass two

Kayakers exploring Isle Royale share the Lake Superior waters with the brawny Ranger III *ferry.*

lighthouses and head out for a close-up look at nearby freighters (906/289-4437).

FESTIVALS
In Copper Harbor, art, music and food take center stage at Art in the Park in mid-August. For a taste of the town's winter fun, come to the Keweenaw Ride-In in early March. Houghton hosts the Bridge Fest and Seafood Fest the second week of June, with food and music on

a parking deck over-looking the Portage Lift Bridge. Head to Chassell the second week of July to mark the sweet and juicy harvest at Strawberry Festival. For information about area celebrations, contact: Keweenaw Tourism Council (800/338-7982).

WINTER ACTIVITIES

One of the snowiest spots in the Midwest, the Keweenaw revels in the huge lake-effect snowfalls created by Lake Superior—often between 300 and 400 inches in a season. Snowmobilers consider the Keweenaw Peninsula among the finest destinations in the country. For information and maps about the region's well-marked routes, contact: Keweenaw Tourism Council (800/338-7982).

Cross-country skiing and snowshoeing also rank high. Many routes take you to pristine backcountry, but if you go, make sure you know the area and have a partner. Skiers also frequent the fine Swede-town Trails south of Calumet, with 18 miles of groomed trails, and the Copper Harbor Ski Trails, with loops around Lake Fanny Hooe, Estivant Pines and the old Clark Mine. Contact: Keweenaw Tourism Council (800/338-7982).

OTHER PLACES TO VISIT IN THE AREA

Isle Royale National Park—Houghton and Copper Harbor are Michigan's gateways to Isle Royale National Park, a rugged and roadless wilderness archipelago of 200 islands in northwestern Lake Superior. The largest, 45-mile-long Isle Royale, attracts backpackers to its 165 miles of hiking trails. Boaters come to explore the ragged shorelines. Trails such as the Greenstone Ridge and Ojibway Loop wind past narrow fjordlike inlets, along rocky cliffs and boggy lowlands, where you're likely to spot one of the island's resident moose. Day hikers stay at park service lodgings in Rock Harbor. Backpack farther afield and you may hear the howl of the elusive timber wolves that roam the island's most remote areas. For information about Isle Royale programs, camping and transpor-tation (via ferry or sea-plane) contact: Isle Royale National Park (906/482-0984).

Porcupine Mountains Wilderness State Park— The largest of Michigan's excellent state parks, the "Porkies" are a hiker's mecca. This vast preserve of virgin

timber, secluded lakes and streams covers 60,000 acres in the northwest corner of the Upper Peninsula, 65 miles southwest of Houghton. More than 90 miles of trails seesaw through virgin tracts of hemlocks and over some rather mountainous terrain. The park's Summit Peak rises to 1,958 feet. Favorite hiking routes include the Escarpment Trail, which winds along a high bluff above the picture-postcard Lake of the Clouds. The East and West River trails, which parallel the rushing Presque Isle River, froth with falls before it empties into Lake Superior. Camp in the park at modern camp-grounds with hookups; at four rustic camping areas accessible by car, but without services; at hike-in rustic cabins or in the backcountry. To reserve a cabin or for information about state parks, contact: Porcupine Mountains Wilderness State Park (906/885-5275). To reserve campsites, call Michigan State Parks' central reservation system (800/44-PARKS). For motels, contact: Western UP Convention & Visitors Bureau (906/932-4850).

By Tina Lassen

MARQUETTE, MICHIGAN

Tucked among the lakeshore's natural wonders, one of upper Michigan's largest cities surprises visitors.

T he city of Marquette reigns over a domain of splendid hills, swift trout streams and a temperamental inland sea. In spring and summer, she's enthroned among fragrant wildflowers in fields of green; in the autumn, she basks in blazing scarlet and gold; in winter, she's wrapped in a blanket of snowy white.

This city of almost 20,000 embraces a wide harbor on the south shore of Lake Superior about halfway between the eastern and westernmost points of Michigan's Upper Peninsula (UP). More than 400 miles northwest of Detroit, the largest city in the UP combines San Francisco's steep hills, Maine's icy waters and Oregon's rocky shoreline.

Marquette's vast blue front yard, Lake Superior, is compelling. Too wide to see across, it's a great freshwater sea. Swimmers brave the waters, though lake temperatures usually are chilling. Sailors thrill to its brisk breezes, anglers rejoice in its whitefish and lake trout, and beachcombers tirelessly retrieve agates from its sandy shores.

The City of Iron

Marquette boasts the ethnic flavor of a blended population that dates to its founding in 1844. Immigrants worked iron, gold and silver mines, and harvested thick forests to feed a thriving timber industry. Iron mining and logging still sustain the economy here. Iron-ore docks jut into the harbor on long pilings, and carefully managed tree farms stretch along the highways.

Local history buffs will happily tell you the story of Marquette's days as an iron boomtown. William Burt, hired by Michigan to survey the state, was nearing the mouth of the Carp River when his compass began spinning wildly. A Chippewa chief led Burt down a trail 10 miles west to the shores of Teal Lake. There, he showed him iron clinging to the roots of an upturned stump. Word of the find spread rapidly, prospectors rushed north, and the city of Marquette sprang up in the wilderness.

You can learn about the area's iron heritage at the Michigan Iron Industry Museum in nearby

TRAVEL MICHIGAN

Marquette's bright red lighthouse.

Negaunee, then tour a real processing mill at the Cleveland-Cliffs Iron Company in nearby Ishpeming. At the ore loading docks in Marquette, oceangoing freighters from around the world pull in to load ore from the rail cars high above.

Art and Architecture

When the snow season ends, Marquette blooms. Petunias and geraniums cascade from window boxes, and sidewalk planters overflow with color. Stroll downtown streets, and you'll discover art galleries nestled beside harbor cafes and corner delis. Wander into the Wattsson and Wattsson jewelry store to see mineral and mining displays and a walk-through replica of an underground mine tunnel. At the end of the tunnel, skilled jewelers work in a glass-enclosed lab, turning raw materials into wearable art.

Across the street, Superior View Studio displays a collection of antique cameras. You can purchase historic photos from the small art gallery. (To find more vintage wares, stop at the convention and visitors bureau for information about antiques shops.)

Not far away, wrought-iron gates lead to the Marquette County Courthouse with its timeworn steps and handsome pink granite porch columns. The courthouse of native brownstone was featured in the 1959 Otto Preminger movie *Anatomy of a Murder*, written by Marquette County native John Voelker (Robert Traver).

Dominating Marquette's skyline is the giant Superior Dome, a 5.1-acre, 14-story upside-down wooden bowl. Check here for a schedule of sporting events, concerts and festivals held at this arena. It's one of the world's largest such domes; daily tours are available.

For an overview of the city and county, consider Marquette Country Tours. After a tour through downtown, you'll head to maple-shaded East

The setting sun silhouettes Miner's Castle at Pictured Rocks National Lakeshore.

JOHN STRAUSS

TOM BUOHKOE

Fishing is fine near the Huron Mountains' Hill's Falls.

Ridge Street for a look at the elaborate mansions built from 1860 to 1900 by Marquette's early elite—mining captains, lumber barons and store owners. Side streets are canopied in trees and dotted with mini-parks and playgrounds.

Looking to The Water

Along Marquette's harbor, the fiery red 1866 lighthouse crowning a rocky outcropping is listed in the National Register of Historic Places. It's one of the most photographed along the Great Lakes. Before the lighthouse was remodeled in 1906, it was said to be patterned after a Franciscan friary in Spain.

Nearby, the Marquette Maritime Museum is dedicated to the ships and sailors who plied the Lake Superior waters. Displays include the birch bark canoe that Charles T. Harvey used to build the first Soo Lock at Sault Ste. Marie.

A narrow neck of land connects Presque Isle, a 328-acre north-woods forest, to the mainland. Follow self-guided paths here to see outdoor sculptures standing among tall native pines and hardwoods.

For a picnic, plan to take along some pasties, which have been a UP tradition since Cornish immigrants first carried them to the mines as an easy-to-eat meal. Save a bit of the crust, and you can feed begging herring gulls from the breakwater. At day's end, linger at Presque Isle's Sunset Point to watch the sun cut a crimson path across the whitecapped waters.

Northwest of Marquette, the Huron Mountains stretch for about 75 miles. Some peaks loom like medieval castles above Lake Superior; gentler slopes dip to white sand beaches that beckon swimmers. Pick up a visitor's map to find tiny communities tucked into the wilderness, paths that climb forested ridges rising more than 1,500 feet and trails that take you into deep valleys to view tumbling waterfalls.

Thick forests cut by 400 miles of rivers, trout streams and dozens of waterfalls surround Marquette. John Voelker, who penned numerous fishing books and mystery novels, was fond of saying that brook trout only live in beautiful places. Anglers who wade in the crystal waters here agree, returning each year to coax the native fish to jump to the fly and make reels sing.

Planning Your Trip to Marquette

Many outdoor attractions in the Marquette area are closed in cold weather months. For more information, contact: Marquette Country Convention & Visitors Bureau (800/544-4321); Upper Peninsula Travel & Recreation Assoc. (800/562-7134).

LODGINGS

Holiday Inn and Comfort Suites are among the chain motels along US-41. Other choices: Landmark Inn, Marquette—This full-service hotel overlooks the harbor. Doubles from $85 (888/7-LANDMARK).

Pine Wood Lodge—Twenty-seven miles east of Marquette near Au Train, this bed and breakfast stands among tall white pines and Lake Superior dunes. From its decks, watch the lights of the aurora borealis dance across the bay. Doubles from $75 (906/892-8300).

DINING

Sweetwater Cafe—This casual eatery offers a multicultural menu with homemade breads fresh from the bakery (906/226-7009).

The Vierling Saloon and Sample Room—This fine-dining restaurant features Lake Superior whitefish fresh from the waters below its hilltop site (906/228-3533). Taste a Marquette favorite, the pasty, at Jean-Kay's (906/228-5310) or Papa Paul's (906/225-0310).

ATTRACTIONS & TOURS

Michigan Iron Industry Museum—In nearby Negaunee, operate hands-on displays: Pull a handle and watch as tiny iron pellets pour down chutes into a waiting miniature freighter (906/475-7857).

Cleveland-Cliffs Iron Company—This Ishpeming firm provides a firsthand look at its active processing mill during the summer (906/486-4841).

Superior Dome—Visit the world's largest wooden dome on the campus of Northern Michigan University (906/227-2850).

U.S. National Ski Hall of Fame and Museum—Skiing in America was born in Ishpeming when Scandinavian miners first leaped from surrounding hills on wooden skis fashioned from barrel staves. See trophies and Olympic skiing highlights (906/485-6323).

Marquette Country Tours—Board the bus and listen as local experts point out significant sites and recount Marquette's history (906/226-6167).

Uncle Ducky's Charters—Angle for whitefish and lake trout, or join a sightseeing tour of lighthouses and islands (906/228-5447).

SHOPPING

Michigan Fair—Irresistible souvenirs abound in a gift shop stocked with all-Michigan products. Owner Leslie White drove from Illinois to Marquette on vacation 20 years ago and stayed (906/226-3894).

Superior View Studio—Visit this intriguing photography museum, gallery and photographic archive (906/225-1952).

Wattsson & Wattsson—See custom-made jewelry fashioned on the spot (906/228-5775).

Thill's Fishery—Try smoked whitefish fresh from Lake Superior (906/226-9851).

FESTIVALS

Art on the Rocks—This juried fine arts-and-crafts festival happens the last weekend in July at Presque Isle Park (906/225-1952; 906/942-7865).

Upper Peninsula 200—The UP 200-mile sled dog race takes place in February. Downtown streets close for the three-day event, which takes mushers on a wide swing through the UP (800/544-4321).

AREA DRIVES & OUTDOOR RECREATION

Northwest of Marquette in the Huron Mountains, hike Sugarloaf Mountain or drive to the top of Mount Marquette (800/544-4321). Keep an eye out for wild game. You may surprise a whitetail deer or an occasional bear or moose. Request a moose-locator map from the Marquette Country Convention & Visitors Bureau (800/544-4321). For more lakeside vistas,

known shipwrecks. Here, at the Alger Underwater Preserve, you can scuba dive or view the submerged wrecks from the glass bottom of the Grand Island Shipwreck tour boat (906/387-4477). Munising, 12 miles east of Au Train, is the headquarters for the Hiawatha Pictured Rocks Visitors Information Center (906/387-3700). Soaring dunes and sandstone cliffs rise as

of a face or the image of a soaring bird—the pictures that help give the lakeshore its name. Superior's pounding has carved more than a dozen fanciful sculptures, from Miner's Castle to Chapel Rock, along the route. Paths lead to landmarks along the shore.

A good choice for lunch or dinner in Munising is Dogpatch (906/387-9948). Friday nights feature seafood buffets, Saturday is prime rib night and Sunday brings diners out for a generous brunch. While you're in town, browse the quirky three-story bookstore, 84 Charing Cross, Eh? (906/387-3937). For a unique north-woods experience, head to the family-owned Iverson Snowshoe Factory off State-28 near Shingleton and watch artisans make snowshoes (906/452-6370).

JOHN STRAUSS

At Au Train, east of Marquette, a sandy beach marks the meeting of the Au Train River and Lake Superior.

drive east on state State-28 for 29 miles to Au Train. At the mouth of the Au Train River, you can swim or build sand castles. Upstream, you can rent a canoe.

OTHER PLACES TO VISIT IN THE AREA
Munising

Driving down the curving hill at Munising (population: 2,800), you might never suspect that in the snug harbor below lie more than 10

high as 200 feet above Lake Superior along a stretch of more than 40 miles to the east of Munising. For a close look at the cliffs along the park's western edge, board the tour boats of Pictured Rocks Cruises (906/387-2379). You'll hear the captain explain that minerals in water seeping from ancient sandstone paint the rocks in ever-changing hues. Look closely and you may see the outline

Seney

Thirty-five miles east along US-2, the old logging town of Seney once rivaled any shoot-'em-up town of the wild west. The crossroads village is now home to the 96,000-acre Seney National Wildlife Refuge (906/586-9851). There's a self-guided driving trail, more than 50 miles of backwoods bicycling and hiking trails and glimpses of wildlife. Near the refuge entrance along State-77, Northland Outfitters (906/586-9801) rents bikes to pedal the 70 miles of trails. Mallards and trumpeter swans (two of the more than 200 types of feathered creatures that stop here) glide in tranquil pools, hardly noticing human intruders. Canoeists put in at Northland for floats on the Manistique River along the refuge's east edge, pulling into the banks at a rustic campsite for lunch or overnight. "It's just you and the backcountry," says Northland owner Tom Gronback. "You want time to stand still."

Grand Marais

Take time to travel 25 miles north on State-77 to Grand Marais and the eastern terminus of Pictured Rocks National Lakeshore (906/387-3700). The quaint lakeside village has small restaurants, cottages and campgrounds.

Follow the signs to Grand Sable Falls, where the river cascades down sandstone banks. To the east, the Grand Sable Dunes reach heights of more than 200 feet, with overlooks and sweeping views of the lake and dunes. Another route 8 miles east takes you to century-old Au Sable

Lighthouse. For an overnight stay not far from the lighthouse, consider Welker's Lodge, a friendly family resort/motel with 51 units. Doubles from $55 (906/494-2361).

Tahquamenon Falls

Back on State-28, turn north at Newberry on State-123. Drive through the sleepy little town north for 30 miles to Tahquamenon Falls State Park, a 40,000-acre wilderness (906/492-3415). Down a wooded path, a low

hike to the gorge, then descend wooden steps to a mist-engulfed platform. Four miles downstream at the lower falls, the river splits into five tamer cascades. Visitors can rent boats and row across a wide pool to the island that separates the falls. Camping sites are available.

A short hike from the upper falls, you'll find Camp 33, a restaurant, brew pub and gift shop (906/492-3341). Tahquamenon Falls tours also are available from The Toonerville Trolley in Soo Junction (906/876-

Boat tours through the Soo Locks in Sault Ste. Marie, Michigan, bring passengers close to the action.

rumble builds to a roar, as if a freight train were hurtling toward you. At the river's edge, the trees part, and a billowing curtain of golden-colored water looms into view—200 feet wide and plunging 50 feet. This is the upper Tahquamenon, among the wildest falls between the Rockies and Niagara. Visitors can

2311 or 888/77TRAIN) and from Tom Sawyer Riverboat and Paul Bunyan Train in Hulbert (906/876-2331). Both towns are off State-28.

Area Museums

North through the village of Paradise along Lake Superior, follow Whitefish Point Road for 11 miles to the Great Lakes Shipwreck

Museum and Whitefish Point Lighthouse (906/635-1742). Displays and salvaged gear tell the stories of ships and the men who never returned from the watery depths. You can't help shivering as you listen to the last recorded radio message from the captain of the *Edmund Fitzgerald*, the giant freighter that went down in a November storm in 1975. The Fitzgerald's bell is prominently displayed as a memorial to her lost crew. Along the shore, beachcombers hunt for colorful lake-smoothed agates and bits of twisted driftwood. There's also the Whitefish Point Bird Observatory, with an interesting gift shop specializing in items depicting nature. The point is one of North America's most important spring flight corridors for raptors. To visit a museum depicting the life of lightkeepers in the 1930s, take the winding Curley Lewis Highway east to the Point Iroquois Lighthouse (906/437-5272). You can climb the 72 steps spiraling to the tower for a dizzying view, then take the boardwalk to the long stretch of sandy beach where wildflowers blossom on low dunes.

Sault Ste. Marie

A historic tale of Great Lakes Indians, fur traders, voyageurs, missionaries and the world's busiest locks is told in this city of 15,000 along St. Mary's River where Lake Superior and Lake Huron meet. It's Michigan's oldest city: Indians had been camping here for generations when French voyageur Etienne Brule paddled to its shores around 1620.

The best place to begin is at the River of History Museum (906/632-1999) where a white path wanders through exhibits and dioramas that portray more than 8,000 years of river history. There's more to see at the Tower of History (906/632-3658). Take the elevator up 21 floors for a panoramic view of the city, locks, St. Mary's Rapids, International Bridge and Sault Ste. Marie, Ontario, across the river.

At the Soo Locks (800/647-2858), climb the observation platform for a ringside view of the best show in town. Sailors line the decks as workers on the locks scurry to secure lines to raise and lower ocean-going freighters, along with tour and pleasure boats. Board the Soo Locks Boat Tours (800/432-6301) for a trip through the locks and past the Algoma Steel Plant on the Canadian side. The Soo Locks Tour Train will take you on a narrated tour through the city and on into Canada (800/387-6200).

LODGINGS

Ojibway Hotel—This renovated landmark overlooking the Soo Locks has 71 rooms and suites, plus the renowned white-linen Freighters restaurant. Doubles from $126 (906/632-4100).
The Water Street Inn—This red brick Queen Anne bed and breakfast overlooks St. Mary's River. Doubles from $75 (800/236-1904).

DINING

Abner's—Come hungry for breakfast or dinner at the longest buffet-bar in town 906/632-4221).
Antlers—Enjoy family dining in this rustic old bar with taxidermy specimens and early American memorabilia decorating the walls and ceiling (906/632-3571).

SHOPPING

Portage Avenue Shops—A four-block line of shops parallels the locks and river. They include lots of local art, plus souvenirs the kids will love (800/647-2858).

By Dixie Franklin

LAKE MICHIGAN'S WEST SHORE

Lake Michigan is the third largest of the Great Lakes and the only one wholly within the U.S. Shaped like a giant teardrop, the lake dips deep into the Heartland, stretching 307 cool blue miles north to south. Along its western shore, Lake Michigan hugs Wisconsin's east edge, lapping at the state's gently rolling farmland, scooping out fine harbors for its port cities and daily renewing the golden ribbon of sand along its beaches.

As the lake exits Wisconsin, it takes a big bite off the northeastern corner of Illinois, skimming along a string of posh suburbs and blessing Chicago with cooler-near-the-lake summer breezes that take the sting out of sidewalk-sizzling temperatures and steambath humidity.

The lake curves east as it leaves Chicago, resting the broad curve of its south shore on Indiana's northwestern shoulder. Over millennia, the lake has left its imprint here, a stirring landscape of sand dunes, bogs and forests that moved poet Carl Sandburg to write "The dunes are to the Midwest what the Grand Canyon is to Arizona and the Yosemite is to California. They constitute a signature of time and eternity."

Read on to learn more about the Indiana Dunes, the villages of Wisconsin's Door County, Milwaukee's summer-long schedule of festivals and Chicago's lakefront charms, all waiting for you along Lake Michigan's western shore.

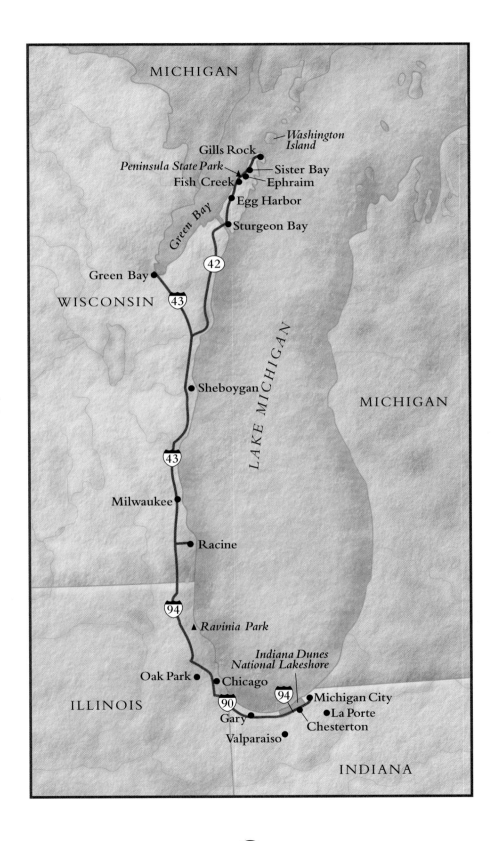

MICHIGAN

Washington Island

Gills Rock

Peninsula State Park — Sister Bay
Fish Creek — Ephraim

Egg Harbor

Sturgeon Bay

Green Bay

42

Green Bay

WISCONSIN 43

Sheboygan

LAKE MICHIGAN

MICHIGAN

43

Milwaukee

Racine

94

▲ *Ravinia Park*

Indiana Dunes National Lakeshore

Oak Park ● Chicago

ILLINOIS 94 Michigan City

90 ● La Porte

Gary Chesterton

Valparaiso

INDIANA

DOOR COUNTY

Picturesque villages line the 250-mile shoreline of the "Cape Cod of the Midwest."

Thrust into Lake Michigan like an uplifted arm, Wisconsin's Door Peninsula is a vacationland defined by water. More than 250 miles of shoreline etch this irregular spit of land in the northeastern corner of the state, with the sheltered waters of Green Bay to the west and the vast expanse of Lake Michigan to the east. Anywhere on the 70-mile-long peninsula, you're just minutes from a water view.

Door County—the entire peninsula is referred to by the name of the county that covers most of it—lives up to its description as the Midwest's Cape Cod. On the lively bay side, amiable villages dot the shoreline. Pleasure boats rock gently in marinas just steps from main streets with shops and galleries ripe for browsing and restaurants serving fresh whitefish pulled from local waters.

Local custom holds that whitefish tastes best when tossed in a big iron pot with potatoes and onions, then boiled outdoors over an open fire and downed with a Wisconsin-brewed beer. Look for restaurants advertising "fish boils" and eat heartily.

On the quieter lake side, the surf pounds rocky limestone cliffs and deserted beach coves. Inland, the landscape broadens into fields of sunflowers and tidy dairy farms. Holsteins munch alfalfa next to sturdy stone walls neatly enclosing hay fields. In nearby orchards, cherry and apple trees line up in perfect rows, clinging to the thin layer of topsoil on this rocky land like petunias in a flower box.

Opening the Door

The village of Sturgeon Bay serves as the unofficial gateway to the peninsula. It was here that a channel linking the bay and lake opened in 1881, creating a bustling port and shipyard. Shipbuilding remains a mainstay of this community of 9,400, the birthplace of giant freighters and sleek yachts. A new maritime museum along the channel chronicles the region's livelihood on the water.

Follow US-42 up the gentle Green Bay shore, and one by one the boxy white frame buildings and graceful church spires of Egg Harbor, Fish Creek, Ephraim and Sister Bay come into view. These bayfront towns whir with activity on sunny summer afternoons, with visitors strolling through galleries bright with the output of glass-makers and watercolor artists. Cafe owners scrub outdoor tables, soon filled

BUCK MILLER

A sailboat
greets dawn on
the quiet waters
of Door County.

by weary shoppers who re-energize with slices of Door County cherry pie.

Maples arch overhead in popular Fish Creek, and blazing red petunias and impatiens seem to line every walkway. At Founder's Square, a dozen or so shops occupy original and reconstructed settlers' buildings scattered along a shady cedar-bark path. A favorite is the Stone Cutter lapidary shop. Crowded with exotic rocks gathered from India to Africa, the Stone Cutter is housed in a creaking, slightly listing cabin, the original homestead of one of Fish Creek's founders, Asa Thorp.

At the town's outskirts, a massive limestone headland juts into the island-studded waters of Green Bay. Lace up a pair of hiking boots or rent a sturdy mountain bike to explore Peninsula State Park, the state's largest. The 5.1-mile gravel Sunset Trail dips among birches and pines and along tranquil Tennison Bay; you may even surprise a shy fawn or an industrious beaver.

Scale the park's 75-foot observation tower for a breathtaking panorama of Horseshoe Island, Eagle Harbor and the hazy horizon of Michigan's Upper Peninsula in the distance. Volunteers give tours of the Eagle Bluff light, a butter-yellow brick tower built in 1868.

Halfway up the Peninsula

Peninsula State Park stretches all the way to Ephraim (pronounced "EE-frum"), one of Door County's most popular vacation communities. Curving around the belly of Eagle Harbor, Ephraim looks as crisp and tidy as a starched white shirt. Snow-white church spires poke through the treetops, and simple, solid inns and homes step down the hill to the waterfront and the bright white sails of boats bobbing in the bay.

The town's simple white architecture originated with the Norwegians who settled the tiny enclave in the 1850s. Take a short walk up the hill to see the Ephraim Moravian Church, a century-old Moravian cemetery and the 1869

The fish boil at White Gull Inn in Fish Creek.

BUCK MILLER

BUCK MILLER

Ephraim's hillside homes look out on Green Bay.

Pioneer Schoolhouse. Looping back down to the bay, you'll spot the rustic and graffiti-covered Anderson Dock and General Store, built in 1859. For decades, captains docking here would scrawl their vessels' names on the weathering wood of the old store.

Across the peninsula, at Whitefish Dunes State Park, ancient dunes rise 90 feet above Lake Michigan, their delicate grasses clinging to the sand, bowing with the breeze. Park trails head north to Cave Point County Park where caves pierce limestone bluffs. On calm days, Lake Michigan's endless blue swell gently nudges the steep faces. When east winds blow, waves heave against the rocks with a roar, shattering into dramatic sprays of white foam.

Two Islands, Two Ferries

At "the top of the thumb," as locals call the tip of the peninsula, is the stalwart fishing community of Gill's Rock. A puffing smokehouse fills the brisk air with the heavy scent of chubs, part of the day's commercial catch. Sportfishing thrives, too, with world-record catches of steelhead and salmon. Early each morning, charter boats lined with whiplike rods set out for "deep-sea" fishing.

Near the working fishing port, a passenger ferry chugs off for the 6-mile trip to Washington Island, a mellow landscape of farms and wildflowers that's perfect for cycling.

The 36-mile Washington Island includes the nation's first Icelandic settlement, and descendants of those original settlers live here today. A tiny commercial fishing community operates at Jackson Harbor, where you'll find a small maritime museum housed in two old fishing sheds.

At Jackson Harbor, a smaller ferry, the *Karfi*, makes the short hop to Rock Island. At the turn of the century, this tiny wooded isle served as the private retreat of Icelander and wealthy inventor Chester Thordarson. Retiring here in 1910, he constructed, stone by stone, a magnificent limestone great hall and boat house. Today, both buildings remain in excellent condition, devoted entirely to a state park. They are the only man-made structures on the island.

Rock Island State Park is a fine retreat for campers and hikers, with 40 primitive campsites, 10 miles of hiking trails, plenty of quiet stone beaches and no motorized vehicles. Hike the Thordarson Loop Trail to the Potawatomi Lighthouse—the northernmost point of Door County and a fitting end to a Door adventure.

Planning Your Visit to Door County

For more information, contact: Door County Chamber of Commerce, 1015 Green Bay Rd., Box 406, Sturgeon Bay, WI 54235-0406 (920/743-4456 or http://doorcounty vacations.com).

LODGINGS

Choose from chain motels, historic bed and breakfasts, vacation cottages, condominiums and full-service resorts throughout the peninsula. The Door County Innline provides up-to-date information about vacancies. Contact: Door County Chamber of Commerce (920/743-4456) or the Innline on the Internet (http://doorcounty vacations.com). Consider these accommodations:

The Barbican—Stay in guest rooms with private baths in a trio of historic homes near Sturgeon Bay's business district. Doubles from $120 (920/743-4854).

The White Lace Inn— "Whimsical Victorian" is how owners Dennis and Bonnie Statz describe the decor of their 1903 inn, a Door County favorite in Sturgeon Bay. Doubles from $98, including breakfast (920/743-1105).

Bay Shore Inn—In Sturgeon Bay, guests at this waterfront resort along Green Bay enjoy one- and two-bedroom suites with kitchens and whirlpools, along with a sand beach, indoor and outdoor pools and more. Doubles from $165 (800/556-4551).

Glidden Lodge—One- to three-bedroom condominiums are located along a secluded stretch of Lake Michigan shore near Jacksonsport, with private beach and indoor pool. From $180 (888/281-1127).

The Blacksmith Inn Bed and Breakfast—In downtown Baileys Harbor, rooms with private baths are above a renovated, working 1912 blacksmith shop. Whirlpools, fireplaces and waterfront views. Doubles from $125 (800/769-8619).

Gordon Lodge—On a quiet point north of Baileys Harbor, cottages and motel units cluster at the mouth of North Bay. Doubles from $120 (800/830-6235).

Harbor House Inn—This gingerbread Victorian and two cottages in Gill's Rock have turn-of-the-century furnishings, a private beach and hot tub. Doubles from $55 (920/854-5196).

Hotel du Nord—In this Sister Bay lodge, some bay-view rooms offer kitchenettes. There are an outdoor pool and whirlpool. Doubles from $89 (800/582-6667).

The Whistling Swan— This meticulously restored clapboard inn in the heart of Fish Creek is one of Door County's earliest lodgings. Doubles from $99 (920/868-3442).

The Ephraim Inn—A lovely starched-white building houses this tidy inn overlooking Eagle Harbor. Doubles from $89 (800/622-2193).

The Landing—A wooded setting in the heart of Egg Harbor offers one- to three-bedroom suites, tennis courts and indoor/outdoor pools. Doubles from $107 (920/868-3282).

Alpine Inn and Cottages— Amenities at this shoreline resort near Egg Harbor include rooms, cottages, a 27-hole golf course and tennis. Doubles from $69 (920/868-3000).

CAMPING

Path of Pines—Near Peninsula State Park in Fish Creek, all sites have hookups. Rec room and heated bathhouse are available (800/868-7802).

Wagon Trail Campground—Seventy acres border Lake Michigan and Mink River Estuary east of Ellison Bay, with separate tent and RV areas (920/854-4818).

State Parks—Three state parks, all bordering

the water, provide sites with or without hookups: Potawatomi State Park, Sturgeon Bay (920/746-2890); Peninsula State Park, Fish Creek (920/868-3258); and Rock Island State Park, northeast of Washington Island (920/847-2235). A fourth, Newport State Park, east of Ellison Bay, has hike-in-only tent sites (920/854-2500).

DINING

The Cookery—Enjoy inventive dishes with local fruits and flavors homemade granola and cherry-stuffed French toast. Fish Creek (920/868-3517).

Inn at Cedar Crossing—This fine restaurant in a historic downtown Sturgeon Bay inn serves local specialties such as capered whitefish (920/743-4249).

Sister Bay Bowl—This no-frills local favorite is known for its lake perch and whitefish (920/854-2841).

Mission Grille—Dine outdoors in this renovated church in Sister front in Sturgeon Bay, the Door County Maritime Museum re-creates a shipbuilder's workshop, exhibits a refurbished pilot's house from the steamer Elba and displays artifacts from sunken ships and more. Open daily year-round (920/743-5958).

Peninsula Players Theatre—Billing itself as the country's oldest resident professional summer stock company, the well-regarded Peninsula Players bring outdoor Broadway

Cyclists in Door County can explore quiet lanes through farmlands or travel the paved roads and trails in Peninsula State Park and on Washington Island.

such as pork tenderloin with cherry chutney and terrific homemade soups in Fish Creek (920/868-3634).

The White Gull Inn—Renowned for its fish boil, many think this popular spot also serves the best breakfast on the peninsula, including Bay (920/854-9070).

Town Hall Bakery—Try sandwiches, salads and tantalizing baked goods in Jacksonport's—you guessed it—old town hall (920/823-2116).

SIGHTSEEING

Door County Maritime Museum—On the water- productions to the shores of Green Bay (920/868-3287).

Birch Creek Music Performance Center—East of Egg Harbor, summer school students from the center present 30 evening concerts mid- June through mid-August. Professional musicians perform in a century-old renovated barn/concert hall (920/868-3763).

Door Community Auditorium—This fine facility in Fish Creek serves as a year-round center for the arts, with guests artists such as Johnny Cash, Leo Kottke and the Minnesota Ballet (920/868-2728).

OUTDOOR ADVENTURES

Peninsula State Park— This 3,700-acre park stretches from Fish Creek to Ephraim, with 19 miles of hiking trails, nearly 500 campsites, bicycling on paved roads and trails, and 10 miles of mountain bike trails. Rent bikes and mopeds at Edge of Park Rentals (920/868-3344). After January 1, book a tee time for the highly acclaimed and highly popular Peninsula Park Golf Course (Box 275, Fish Creek, WI 54212). Reservations also may be made by phone 7 days or less in advance (920/854-5791).

The Ridges Sanctuary— Named for the ancient sand ridges formed along the Lake Michigan shore, this 1,000-acre preserve north of Baileys Harbor is home to an outstanding variety of wildflowers, including 25 kinds of orchids. Learn more with a naturalist-led tour or self-guided hike, then relax

on the fine sand beach. Trail fee required (920/839-2802).

Washington and Rock island ferries and tours— A 30-minute ferry ride from Gill's Rock or Northport brings passengers to Washington Island, a haven crisscrossed by flat and lightly traveled roads that are popular with cyclists. Washington Island Ferry Line for cars and passengers (800/223-2094); *Island Clipper* for passengers only; narrated Washington Island tours available (920/854-

2972). From Washington Island, ferry to Rock Island State Park (920/847-2235).

Newport State Park— With the popularity of Peninsula State Park, this excellent park on the lake side of Door

County (5 miles east of Ellison Bay) is sometimes overlooked. However, it boasts wonderful hiking on 28 miles of trails, some along the rocky shoreline, others past sand ridges, bogs and inland Europe Lake. Beachcombers and sunbathers enjoy the 3,000-foot sand beach. Camp at 16 backpack-in sites only (920/854-2500).

Whitefish Dunes State Park—Follow the Red Trail to an observation deck on Old Baldy, the park's tallest dune, to

Door County's 250 miles of shoreline include long solitary stretches of sand along Lake Michigan.

view the grassy mounds that rise as high as 90 feet. The White Trail heads north to Cave Point County Park where eons of pounding water have sculpted tunnels and caves in the limestone bluffs

(920/823-2400).
Mink River Estuary—
Where the Mink River spills into Lake Michigan's Rowley's Bay (southeast of Ellison Bay), a rich wetlands provides a vital spawning area for fish and a migration hideaway for hawks, herons and other birds. Paddling is the best way to explore this quiet Nature Conservancy land of cattails and wild-rice paddies. Launch into the bay at the east end of County-Z.

the Midwest, as world-caliber classical musicians perform in Fish Creek for several weeks each August

ward off cabin fever, with kooky contests such as the kite-powered ski race. Many shops, galleries and restaurants

Door County's woods and meadows inspire the landscapes of Judi Ekholm, an artist in Sister Bay.

FESTIVALS

May marks the Festival of Blossoms, with open houses at galleries, a shipyard tour and a lighthouse walk. Contact: Door County Chamber of Commerce for specifics about this county-wide event (920/743-4456). Ephraim's Fyr Bal Festival in mid-June honors its Scandinavian heritage and marks the summer solstice with bonfires lit along the shore of Eagle Harbor and a rollicking ceremony to chase away winter witches (920/854-5501). Washington Island celebrates its ancestry at the Scandinavian Festival the first weekend in August (920/847-2179). The Peninsula Music Festival attracts symphony devotees from all around

(920/854-4060). Sister Bay draws crowds during Fall Fest, held the second week of October, when the bluffs are ablaze with color (920/854-2812).

WINTER FUN

Door County's state parks offer more than 70 miles of cross-country ski trails, including groomed tracks at Peninsula and Potawatomi state parks. Check with the park offices for dates for candlelight skiing. Downhill thrill-seekers should head for the small alpine ski area at Potawatomi State Park or the steep sledding hills at Peninsula. Ice fishing ranks high on protected bays and inland lakes. In February, Fish Creek hosts the zany Winter Games to

remain open year-round for those seeking a quiet winter getaway.

OTHER PLACES TO VISIT IN THE AREA

It's an easy 45-mile drive south to Green Bay. Make the pilgrimage to the Packer Hall of Fame to view memorabilia, highlight films and those famous Super Bowl trophies (920/499-4281 or 888/4GB PACK). June through August, tours start here to see the Packers' home turf, Lambeau Field, right across the street. For more information, contact: Green Bay Area Visitors & Convention Bureau (920/494-9507 or 888/TO SEE GB).

By Tina Lassen

MILWAUKEE

Celebrate summer with great music and great food in this city of festivals.

Milwaukee's Native American name, "Millioki," means gathering place by the waters. It's an accurate description of southeastern Wisconsin's ethnic melting pot along Lake Michigan and especially appropriate to the 54-acre stretch of shoreline just south of downtown known as the Henry W. Maier Festival Grounds.

The Festival Grounds are celebration central in summertime Milwaukee, the cool lakeside setting for a hot lineup of ethnic celebrations, music extravaganzas, fireworks and circuses. With a festival scheduled almost every weekend from June through September, visitors can count on finding fun all summer long.

Remembering Old-World Roots

Sharon Fleck's dancing feet flirt with the audience as she twirls and hops on the Festival Grounds stage. Performing a traditional Polish shepherd's dance—in which village men preen and bashful beauties demur—Sharon fairly shimmers in her authentic folk costume: a sequin-spangled vest and a crisp-as-paper skirt embroidered with roses. Her brown braids, cinched with bright red ribbons, snap like whips about her smiling face. Grandma Czerwonka would be proud.

It's a scene repeated with tireless energy—and globe-spanning costume changes—throughout the summer. In this sociable city, new generations delight in celebrating old-country traditions.

The sprawling lakefront festival park serenades the city all summer with up-tempo mazurkas, tarantellas, polkas and more—theme music for Polish Fest, Festa Italiana, German Fest and the rest of the rollicking events that light up the Festival Grounds.

More than 45 participating ethnic groups make up much of Greater Milwaukee's population of 1.4 million. Year-round celebrations give each group a chance to parade their costumes, traditions and pride. The granddaddy of them all, November's Holiday Folk Fair, was first held in 1943. These parties reach their zenith in summer. Every weekend, early morning breezes from Lake Michigan waft across the festival park, carrying the exotic and pungent aromas of the world's varied cuisines.

GREATER MILWAUKEE CONVENTION & VISITORS BUREAU

Indian Summer
Festival honors
ancient customs.

The Biggest Fest of All

The crowded calendar of ethnic fests is the legacy of nearly 40 years ago. Back in 1961, Milwaukee's Mayor Maier visited Munich, Germany, and boasted to his counterpart there that not only did Milwaukee's beer beat the best of the German brews, but his city by the lake could stage a summer fair to rival Munich's famed Oktoberfest. And so Summerfest, Milwaukee's 11-day music-and-food extravaganza, was born.

Sandwiched between ethnic festivals, Summerfest's exuberant multistage, something-for-everybody party straddles the last week of June and first week of July. It has grown to be one of the largest musical festivals in the world. Not a salute to any one ethnic culture, the music expo instead celebrates America's broad-based musical tastes.

For almost two weeks, rock bands rub tattooed shoulders with tuxedoed cellists, and down-home country-and-western cowboys help tune mariachi guitars. Big-name acts perform at the 24,000-seat open-air Marcus Amphitheater. Hot local garage bands draw fans to living-room-size stages that hug the boulder-lined lakeshore. Senior citizens arrive by the busloads to twirl to Big Band-era classics played in an airy tent.

Posh downtown cafes, neighborhood restaurants and church groups operate dozens of food booths. The eclectic mix of food and music results in blissful patrons toting paper plates of barbecued ribs and chocolate croissants as they zig-zag from the zydeco stage to the golden-oldies rock venue.

Once Summerfest was established, the city encouraged neighborhood church festivals and others to move to the lakeside locale to keep the festival grounds occupied during the rest of the summer. The Italian community accepted the invitation, a curious city-wide crowd showed up to enjoy the food and fun, and the tradition of summer ethnic festivals was born.

Milwaukeans celebrate their heritage.

WILLIAM HOPKINS

THOMAS LEMKE/THE PICTURE CUBE, INC.

**Seats fill up
when the circus
comes to town.**

Let the Games Begin

The Milwaukee Highland Games kick
off the summer shindigs with kilt-clad
athletes competing as bagpipes drone in a
woodsy park in north-suburban
Glendale. Asian Moon Fest and Polish
Fest are the first major ethnic festivals
of the year at the Festival Grounds,
followed by Festa Italiana, German Fest
and Irish Fest. In late summer and early
autumn, African World Festival, Mexican
Fiesta and the Indian Summer
celebration take the stages. A few blocks
from the lakefront, mid-July Bastille Days
bring Francophiles and just plain fun-
lovers to the streets surrounding East
Town's Cathedral Square area, one of
Milwaukee's prettiest downtown settings.
Zydeco music's biggest stars come up
from Louisiana to play for fans who
dance in the street.

It's worth a trip to the city's west side
(a 15-minute drive from downtown) for
the savory lamb and sweet sticky baklava
at Greek Festival, held on the grounds
of the lovely Frank Lloyd Wright-designed
Annunciation Greek Orthodox church.

Festivals and other summer events—
including the "Big Bang," the spectacular
fireworks display at the lakefront that
kicks off Summerfest—can crowd
nearly 1 million people into
Milwaukee's downtown area. To
accommodate the crush, shuttles pick
up festival-goers from various hotels.
This method of transportation is highly
recommended for getting to and from
the Festival Grounds.

Here Comes
the Circus!

In July, an all-American event unique
to this city—the Great Circus Parade—
comes trumpeting into town from its
year-round home in Baraboo,
Wisconsin, and sets up camp at the
Festival Grounds. Keeping alive the
extravagant spirit of the great big-top
shows, the parade stretches for 4
gleaming miles. Jungle cats caged in
spoke-wheeled wagons exchange
nervous glances with balloon-toting
kids astride parents' shoulders.

Amid the brass-keyed cacophony of a
steam-belching calliope, a nose-to-tail
row of ponderously dignified elephants
lumbers by, their ears fanning at the
onlookers who cram the sidewalks
along Wisconsin Avenue. Snorting teams
of plumed draft horses pull the parades'
star attractions, some 70 colorfully
painted circus wagons.

Planning Your Visit to Milwaukee

For more information, contact: Greater Milwaukee Convention & Visitors Bureau, Inc. (800/231-0903).

LODGINGS

A range of chain hotels and motels serves the Milwaukee area. Lodgings listed here are in or near downtown Milwaukee. Ask about package rates, discounts and lower, off-season rates.

Pfister Hotel—This Victorian grande dame of Milwaukee hostelries dazzles with marble staircases, a stunning barrel-vaulted lobby with fireplace and gracious service. Doubles start at $245 (414/273-8222).

Wyndham Milwaukee Center Hotel—Ask for a room facing the landmark Milwaukee City Hall and you'll have an only-in-Milwaukee view—in the heart of the restaurant and theater district. Doubles from $149 (414/276-8686).

Hyatt Regency Milwaukee—This hotel along the Milwaukee River boasts a soaring atrium lobby, walkways to shopping and convention facilities, and a revolving Polaris restaurant on the top floor. Doubles from $180 (414/276-1234).

Park East Hotel—

Within walking distance of the lake, this small, contemporary hotel in a quiet area north and east of downtown provides free shuttle service to major downtown sites. Doubles from $105 (414/276-8800).

County Clare—This 31-room inn is tucked in a neighborhood of historic homes near downtown and the lake. Rooms have queen-size beds and whirlpool tubs, and the inn's pub boasts a fireplace and stained-glass windows. Doubles from $120 (414/272-5273).

DINING

Karl Ratzsch's—Dirndl-skirted waitresses serve buttery Wiener schnitzel and sauerbraten in gingersnap gravy in this generations-old gathering place that entertains with piano music on weekends (414/276-2720).

Three Brothers—Locals and visiting celebrities trek to Bay View on the city's south side for home-cooked Serbian food. The restaurant is in a 19th-century Schlitz tavern that dates to the time when beer was served in brewery-owned saloons. No credit cards, please (414/481-7530).

King and I—Along the river downtown is one of the most popular of the city's many Thai

restaurants. Subdued decor and thoughtful service by wait staff in authentic costumes. Open for lunch and dinner (414/276-4181).

La Boulangerie Cafe—The lower level of a reclaimed warehouse in Milwaukee's trendy Third Ward just south of downtown houses this brick-walled dining spot. For breakfast, try the sweetly memorable cinnamon-bun French toast; at lunch, unusual pasta salads star (414/271-3900).

Sanford—For fine dining in an intimate, low-key setting, try this former grocery store in a working-class neighborhood. It's nationally recognized for entrées such as elk-loin served with sweet-potato gnocchi and lamb with pine nuts and sultanas (414/276-9608).

SIGHTSEEING

Milwaukee Public Museum—This highly praised natural history museum offers hands-on computer exhibits, a rain forest, dinosaurs and a buffalo stampede (414/278-2702).

Discovery World—See interactive science and technology exhibits. A laser beam show and lively theatricals add zip. The gift shop sells unusual gizmos and games (414/765-0777).

Betty Brin Children's Museum—Toys By Us

lets kids make their own souvenirs; the Ear-y Canal, for example, teaches about hearing. (414/291-0888).

Miller Brewing Company—No trip to Milwaukee is complete without a brewery tour. Year-round tours, noon to 3:30 p.m., Mondays-Saturdays. Call for tour information (414/931-BEER).

Milwaukee County Zoo—The lovable penguins at the Aviary and the impressive

Opened in 1995, Betty Brin Children's Museum is part of a lakefront complex with handy underground parking.

gorilla in the Primate House are crowd-pleasers, as are the petting zoo and the train. It's ranked high among major zoos for its open-air "predator and prey" exhibits (414/256-5412).

Mitchell Park Conservatory—"The Domes" is what locals call these three climate-controlled greenhouses that resemble upside-down glass bowls. Each has a botanical theme:

rain forest, desert and seasonal display (414/649-9800).

FESTIVALS

Contact festival organizers for further information about specific events. Fests not held at the Henry W. Maier Festival Grounds are indicated. Call for the best directions. Also note that most of the festivals charge admission. Once you're inside, entertainment is free.

June

Milwaukee Highland Games—Held annually in June in Old Heidelberg Park, in the northeast suburb of Glendale (414/796-0807). Bagpipes signal the gathering of more than 45 Scottish clans. View caber tossing and other Highland athletics, then dine on bridies (meat pies) and shortbread.

Asian Moon Festival—Held annually in early to

mid-June (414/821-9829). Thai, Chinese, Filipino, Hmong and other of Milwaukee's Asian immigrants re-create their native cultures with music and a marketplace at this poetically named event. Sample sweet banana egg rolls and green beans with spiced pork.

Lakefront Festival of Arts—Held annually in mid-June, Milwaukee Art Museum Grounds, 750 N. Lincoln Memorial Dr. (414/224-3850). This annual juried outdoor arts festival shows the work of 185 artists from across the country. Artist demonstrations and children's events are featured Fridays-Sundays.

Polish Fest—Held the third weekend of June, this annual event features costumed folk dancers (414/529-2140). Take a turn around the nonstop polka stage. Don't leave without sampling the pierogi (cheese-filled pasta pockets), golabki (cabbage rolls) and, of course, kielbasa (spicy Polish sausage).

Summerfest—Held annually late June-early July (414/273-FEST; 800/273-FEST). The celebration includes general admission to the Festival Grounds and reserved tickets for Marcus Amphitheatre.

GREATER MILWAUKEE CONVENTION & VISITORS BUREAU

Shuttle service from off-site parking and hotels is available. 11:30 a.m.–midnight each day.

July

The Great Circus Parade Week—Held annually in July or early August, the parade moves through downtown Milwaukee and along the lakefront (608/356-8341). The circus train pulls in from Baraboo (the original winter quarters of the Ringling Brothers Circus and site of the present Circus World Museum) to the rail yards along the downtown lakefront. Teams of giant draft horses make a show of unloading the circus wagons, which are on display until parade time. On the grounds of the nearby Veterans Park, the royal Hanneford Circus of Sarasota, Florida, stages a dozen big-top performances ($5 admission). For parade viewing tips, check local newspapers. Also see The Greatest Web Site on Earth (www.circus parade.com).
Bastille Days—This commemoration of the French Revolution is held annually in mid-July in East Town (414/271-7400). Jefferson Street is closed off to make room for the food tents and stages of a

lighthearted fest that's a bit more sophisticated than the city's myriad other celebrations. Musicians pump tuneful zydeco music from squeezeboxes, joyous background music to French cuisine and wine tasting. Later, footsteps echo at midnight—thousands of them pounding the downtown streets in the Bastille Day 5-K fun run.
Annunciation Greek Festival—Held annually in mid-July at Annunciation Greek Orthodox Church, 9400 W. Congress, 10 miles northwest of downtown (414/461-9400), the festivities begin with the aroma of roast lamb and chicken. Try the loukomades (small honey puffs topped with cinnamon). Join in exuberant Greek dancing. You may tour the impressive church, one of architect Frank Lloyd Wright's last big commissions.
Festa Italiana—Held

annually in mid- to late-July, this popular fest draws as many as 150,000 visitors (414/223-2193). Sicilian brass bands roam, Venetian gondolas wheel down the streets and platefuls of pizza and pasta are everywhere. At evening's end, fantastic fireworks explode in great showers of red, white and green (the colors of the Italian flag). On Sunday, a Mass is celebrated followed by a solemn procession.
German Fest—Held

Downtown Milwaukee's streets and buildings light up at night, giving the city a festive look year-round.

GREATER MILWAUKEE CONVENTION & VISITORS BUREAU

annually in late July, this is billed as the largest authentic festival of German traditions in North America (414/464-9444; www.germanfest.com). And it's easy to see why. *Ja, spanferkel* is spoken here. Roasted, whole, spitted pigs rotate over glowing coals—nearly 200 are consumed by festival's end. The marketplace boasts baroque beer steins, Black Forest-carved cuckoo clocks and nutcrackers.

Wisconsin State Fair— A memorable experience, the fair takes place in late July and early August at Wisconsin State Fair Park in neighboring West Allis (414/266-7000; 800/884-FAIR). Admire the Holsteins, gobble a cream puff and stay for the dazzling fireworks display.

August

African World Festival— In early August (414/372-4567), tribal priests open the fest by blessing the land and water, then roam a re-created African village during this showcase of African-American culture. Along with native African dances and perfor-mances, there are rap, blues, jazz, gospel and bebop—Africa's rhythms bequeathed to the American culture. A marketplace sells African-made and African-themed wares.

Irish Fest—Held annually the third weekend in August, the "gentle festival" is the largest Irish music and cultural event of its kind in North America (414/476-3378). Enjoy the world's top Irish and Irish-American dancers, musicians, drama, kids' activities, marketplace

and Irish sports, including Gaelic football and hurling.

Serbian Days—This lively event occurs annually in late August at St. Sava Serbian Orthodox Cathedral, 3201 South 51st St. (414/545-4080). Big bands perform, and savory barbecued chicken, lamb and pork top the menu at this big neighborhood church festival.

Mexican Fiesta—Hats off to this annual event in late August (414/383-7066). Participants vie for honors in el baile dance competition, el grito contest and the jalapeño-eating challenge in which contestants consume flaming-hot peppers without a whimper.

September

Indian Summer Festival—Held annually in September, on the weekend following Labor Day, American Indian dancers from tots to elders dress in deerskin, dyed feathers and beads to compete in the Pow-Wow dance events. Before the festival begins, prayers to the spirits of the North, South, East and West bless the site. Along with storytelling and lacrosse demonstrations there are re-creations of tribal villages with longhouses, wigwams and teepees. Sample

venison, buffalo, wild rice and cherry fry pie. Craft areas feature talented artisans who create dolls, carve wooden pipes, and weave rugs and baskets (414/774-7119).

FESTIVALS

Holiday Folk Fair International—Ethnic clubs and church groups plan all year for their parts in this long-established event held in late November at The Midwest Express Center (414/225-6220). Eat your way around the world at the food booths, enjoy authentic music and dance on stage, and admire carefully constructed settings that show customs of native lands. Start your holiday shopping in the marketplace, a bonanza of imported foods and crafts.

Winterfest—Winter fun and frolic happen during December and January (800/231-0903). An Olympic-size skating rink at Cathedral Square is shared by professional figure skaters, as well as families happily scooting across the ice. The annual ice-sculpting contest results in grand and glistening artistic achievements. Experience other exciting venues, too.

By Steve Slack

CHICAGO

Looking better than ever, that toddlin' town along the lake is ready for a fun-packed summer.

This big, boisterous, beautiful, cultured, contentious, down-to-earth Midwest city has lavished its lakefront with treasures. Strung along Chicago's 29-mile-long Lake Michigan shoreline are tree-studded parks, world-class museums, handsome boat harbors, beautifully groomed beaches and the magnificent Buckingham Fountain. Whether cycling, speeding on in-line skates, walking dogs or pushing strollers, Chicagoans head to the lakefront. They invite visitors to do the same.

Any season is a great time to blow into the Windy City, but Chicago is at its best when the temperature, as well as the activity level, sizzles.

Navy Pier
Navy Pier epitomizes Chicago's come-out-and-play attitude. After stretching a cool 3,000 feet into the blue-green lake, the sparkling 50-acre one-time naval training facility dips up something for everyone— a lively children's museum, an IMAX 3-D theater, 36 hand-painted animal figures spinning on a nostalgic carousel, a medley of flowers and fountains, and a 150-foot-high Ferris wheel.

The Ferris wheel's circle of bright red seats dominates the entire pier and is easily visible from Lake Shore Drive, the city's ribbon of asphalt along the lake. The striking white canopy of the Pier's 1,500-seat Skyline Stage invites visitors to stay out late, as sounds of music, theater and dance waft through the evening air.

Strolling performers, dock-side cafes, a beer garden and live bands populate the pier's perimeter. Alongside, a fleet of boats bobs enticingly, inviting you to take to the lake. Choose from dining cruises on luxury yachts, quick trips on speedboats, handy water taxi services, narrated sightseeing excursions and even a leisurely sail on a four-masted schooner.

Grant Park
A half-mile or so south of Navy Pier is "Chicago's front yard," Grant Park. This busy venue for summer fun faces the music. The free Grant Park Music Festival features classical selections under the stars all summer long. In August, blanket-toting jazz lovers stake out choice spots, then relax as cool Lake Michigan breezes carry the sounds of hot jazz across

PETER J. SCHULZ/CITY OF CHICAGO

A short walk from downtown, Navy Pier stretches out into Lake Michigan.

the park's grassy expanse. With the skyline of the Loop (an area defined by a rounded configuration of elevated train tracks—El) as a backdrop, fans chow down thick wedges of Chicago-style pizza and sizzling Polish sausages. From promising young players to jazz legends, the 20-year-old festival draws more than 300,000 jazz enthusiasts.

The big-city version of a block party takes place here, too, as dozens of vendors set up for Taste of Chicago, the annual food extravaganza that brings together Italian sausage and chocolate-dipped frozen bananas, corn dogs and crab legs, lobster tail and *tom yum goong* (shrimp hot and sour soup), turkey legs and tempura—and perhaps heartburn and indigestion.

Museums and Architecture

The Chicago metropolitan area boasts more than 100 museums, dedicated to everything from cookie jars to medieval medical instruments. Some of the most venerable and noteworthy institutions stand stalwartly along the lakefront. The Art Institute, undisputed grande dame of Chicago museums, regales visitors with 40 centuries of creative expression, including renowned Impressionist and post-Impressionist collections. Miniatures loom large: See the perfectly scaled Thorne rooms, tiny dioramas depicting historic interiors. The gift shop's artist-made jewelry and sumptuous coffee table books may inspire you to start your Christmas shopping early. Remember to pat the bronze lions guarding the Art Institute entrance for good luck.

Across Michigan Avenue and three blocks north is the majestic Chicago Cultural Center. Built in 1897 as Chicago's central library, its interior is a breathtaking amalgam of marble, gilt and Tiffany glass. No longer a library, "The People's Palace" now serves as performance space for cultural institutions, as well as a tourist information center. Drop in on one of the many free events or just stop by to admire the space.

A short distance south, dinosaurs reign at The Field Museum; the stars are always out at the Adler Planetarium & Astronomy Museum; and 6,000 sea denizens reside at Shedd Aquarium.

Chicago's architecture—along with its public sculpture—constitutes a city-wide outdoor museum. This is the town

Buckingham Fountain lights up the night.

PETER J. SCHULZ/CITY OF CHICAGO

Sampling ethnic treats at Taste of Chicago.

MICHAEL SLAUGTER

where the skyscraper was born, where Frank Lloyd Wright revolutionized design and where buildings by a who's who of architecture demand attention. This is especially true in the downtown area known as the Loop. In fact, you can take a guided tour of Chicago's Loop architecture from the El—or by foot, bus, boat or bicycle.

Shopping and Other Diversions

If shopping is your bag, zip over to State Street, anchored by the flagship Marshall Field's. (Take time to look at the store's breathtaking Tiffany dome, then stop at the candy counter for a box of Frango mints, the made-right-here chocolate treat that has delighted Chicagoans for generations.) The grand old shopping street has undergone a recent face-lift, including authentic 1920s-style streetlights.

A few blocks east, raised flower beds mark the center of Michigan Avenue, where the "Magnificent Mile" begins at the Chicago River and runs north to Oak Street. The dazzling collection of big-name shops covers the gamut from the high-tech energy of interactive sports and entertainment stores such as

Nike Town and Viacom to the subtle splendor of Tiffany's and Gucci.

Chicago is a city of ethnic neighborhoods, many of the most welcoming just a 5-minute cab ride from downtown. Let your appetite be your guide: Try Italian ices along Taylor Street; dig into *dim sum* in Chinatown (Cermak Road and Wentworth Avenue); go for Greek along Halsted Street, bite into burritos in Pilsen (18th Street and Blue Island); or pig out on pierogi on Milwaukee Avenue in the heart of the city's Polish community.

There are those who hold that the only proper way to celebrate a summer day in Chicago is with a hot dog in hand at Wrigley Field, the nostalgic northside home of the Chicago Cubs, or with the Chicago White Sox at the sleek southside Comiskey Park. When spectator sports pall, plan a workout of your own: Rent a bike or in-line skates and cruise the paved 18-mile lakefront trail that heads north from downtown.

"The Windy City," "City of the Big Shoulders," "The City That Works"— whatever you call it, chances are, just one visit will have you echoing Frank Sinatra's tuneful sentiment: "Chicago is my kind of town."

Planning Your Visit to Chicago

For more information, contact: Chicago Office of Tourism, Chicago Cultural Center, 78 E. Washington St., Chicago, IL 60602 (312/744-2400; http://www. ci.chi.il.us/tourism). For a free visitor information packet, call (800/ 2CONNECT). For hotel reservations, call your favorite hotel or the Illinois Reservation Service (800/491-1800). Visitor Information Centers are located at the Historic Water Tower, 806 N. Michigan Ave.; Chicago Cultural Center, 77 E. Randolph St. (at Michigan Ave.); and Illinois Market Place, Navy Pier (at the extreme east end of Grand Avenue). Listings here are in the downtown area unless otherwise indicated.

LODGINGS

Dozens of hotels put you near the lake and all the action downtown and along North Michigan Avenue. For the best value, always ask about special packages and discounts.

Four Seasons Hotel—Named as America's number one hotel in several polls, this posh hostelry is around the corner from North Michigan Avenue shopping and a short stroll from the lake. Doubles from $420. 120 E. Delaware Pl. (800/332-3442).

Holiday Inn—Accommodations are in the Chicago City Centre, near the fun at Navy Pier. Doubles from $195. 300 E. Ohio St. (312/787-6100).

Palmer House Hilton—This hotel is near the Art Institute and State Street shopping. Doubles from $225. Children under 18 stay free. 17 E. Monroe St. (312/726-7500).

Claridge Hotel—This small hotel is in the chic Near North area. Doubles from $190. 1244 N. Dearborn Pkwy. (800/245-1258).

Best Western Inn of Chicago, Near North—Stay close to Magnificent Mile shops. Doubles from $109. 162 E. Ohio St. at Michigan Ave. (312/787-3100).

DINING

Berghoff's—This century-old treasure is big and bustling with no-nonsense waiters and American/German cuisine. 17 W. Adams (312/427-3170).

Frontera Grill—Taste authentic Mexican dishes prepared by much-praised chef and cookbook author Rick Bayless. Enjoy ethnic flavors and colorful folk art. 445 N. Clark St. (312/661-1434).

Gold Coast Dogs—Don't leave town without sampling a classic Chicago-style hot dog—that means topped with bright green relish and a sprinkling of celery salt. 418 N. State St. and other locations (312/527-1222).

Jerome's Red Ginger—In the Lincoln Park neighborhood north of downtown, this is a favorite for casual Sunday brunch served on a flower-bedecked terrace. 2450 N. Clark St. (773/327-2207).

Kiki's Bistro—Chicago is smitten with casual French eateries—at least a dozen thrive here —including this cozy spot. Classic dishes include country pâtés, mushroom ragoût and escargot Bourgogne. 900 N. Franklin St. (312/335-5454).

Pizzeria Uno—The birth-place of thick, gooey Chicago-style pizza in the 1950s still packs 'em in. 29 E. Ohio St. at Wabash Ave. (312/321-1000).

Pizzeria Due—Uno's sibling, one block away, offers a little less ambience and a little shorter wait. 619 N. Wabash Ave. at Ontario St. (312/943-2400).

Spiaggia—Splurge on award-winning Italian gourmet cuisine while enjoying superb service and fabulous views of North Michigan Avenue and the Oak Street

Beach area. 980 N. Michigan Ave. (312/280-2750).

Cafe Spiaggia— Spiaggia's next-door casual cafe has lavish murals and more moderate prices (312/280-2755). Also look for family-friendly dining opportunities in Chicago's museum cafes, ethnic neighborhoods and vertical shopping malls.

Admire goldwork from the Andes, West African sculptures, American glass and furniture, Chinese bronzes, Greek vases, Korean ceramics, European paintings, architectural drawings, Thorne miniature rooms, paintings, photography— totalling more than 225,000 works of art. Children can attend exhibits, activities and workshops. Donation is

exhibit at O'Hare Airport (312/527-1000).

Chicago Cultural Center— A schedule of films, lectures and live performances pack each day and with few exceptions they're free. Obtain free Loop Tour train tickets here June-October. The Corner Bakery Cafe in the art-covered lobby serves great coffee and snacks. 78 E. Washington St. (312/346-3278 for recorded information or 312/744-2400).

Field Museum—Explore the earth and its people from dinosaurs to world cultures, including Egyptian, African and Oceanic. Free on Wednesdays. Roosevelt Rd. and Lake Shore Dr. (312/922-9410).

Harold Washington Library Center—Looming over the South Loop, this extraordinary collection boasts more than books. Experience lectures, films and performances, and a serene and splendid Winter Garden on the top floor (free). 400 S. State St. (312/747-4300).

WILLIAM HOPKINS

Pack a picnic basket and head up the North Shore to the Ravinia Festival, a summer music tradition.

MUSEUMS PLUS

Adler Planetarium & Astronomy Museum— See the Sky Show and astronomy and space exploration exhibit. Free on Tuesdays, charge for Sky Show. 1300 S. Lake Shore Drive (312/922-STAR).

Art Institute of Chicago—

required; free on Tuesdays. Michigan Avenue at Adams Street (312/443-3600).

Chicago Children's Museum—Learning is fun for kids ages 2–12. 700 E. Grand Ave. at Navy Pier. Free from 5 to 8 p.m. Thursdays. Kids on the Fly is a free satellite

Lincoln Park Zoo—Visit the children's zoo, zoo nursery and a replica of an Illinois farm. Free; charge for parking. Cannon Dr. at Fullerton Ave., a short drive north of the Loop in Lincoln Park (312/742-2000).

Museum of Broadcast Communications—This

TRAVEL GUIDE

is free, except for do-it-yourself newscasts and use of archival tapes. In the Chicago Cultural Center (312/629-6000). Museum of Contemporary Art—Post-1945 paintings, sculptures, photography, videos and other art are housed in this 150,000-square-foot facility with a theater, sculpture garden, restaurant and views of Lake Michigan. Closed Mondays; first Tuesday of the month is free; children 12 and younger admitted free. 220 E. Chicago Ave. (312/280-2660). Museum of Science and Industry—Five miles south of the other major lakefront museums is a majestic building from the 1893 Columbian Exposition. Along with the Omnimax theater and high-tech interactive exhibits are long-time favorites: the realistic coal mine, a World War II German submarine and the ultimate dollhouse, Colleen Moore's Fairy Castle. Free on Thursdays, but Omnimax admission is charged. 57th St. and Lake Shore Dr. (773/684-1414). John G. Shedd Aquarium—A striking simulation of a Pacific Northwest coastal habitat, the world's largest marine mammal pavilion, a Coral Reef tank and other displays introduce visitors to 6,000-plus marine animals. Reduced

admission on Thursdays. 1200 S. Lake Shore Drive (312/939-2438). Terra Museum of American Art—Look for works by Whistler, Cassatt and Wyeth. Closed Mondays; donation is required. Free on Tuesdays and the first Sunday of the month; free to children under 14 and teachers. 666 N. Michigan Ave. (312/664-3939).

ON THE WATERFRONT
Chicago is awash in cruising options. Access these at Navy Pier: Shoreline Sightseeing—narrated tours, also water taxi service (312/222-9328); Odyssey II—the largest fine-dining cruise

Bronze lions guard the steps of The Art Institute of Chicago, a Michigan Avenue landmark.

PETER J. SCHULZ/CITY OF CHICAGO

ship on the Great Lakes (630/990-0800); The Windy—four-masted schooner where passengers help raise and trim the sails and take turns at the wheel (312/595-5555); Seadog—a lakefront speedboat ride

(312/822-7200); Spirit of Chicago—dining and entertainment cruises (312/836-7899). These boats depart from various sites: Chicago from the Lake—for historical and architectural cruises, North Pier (312/527-1977); Wendella Sightseeing Boats—Narrated lake and river tours, Michigan Avenue Bridge and Wrigley Building on the north side of river (312/337-1446); Mercury river and lakefront tours—Michigan Ave. Bridge and Wacker Dr. on the south side of the river (312/332-1353); Chicago's First Lady—description by Chicago

Architecture Foundation docents of buildings seen from the Chicago River. Southwest corner of Michigan Avenue and Wacker Drive (312/922-3432). To cruise alongside the water, see Bike Chicago. Along with classic cycles are mountain bikes, kids' bikes, tandem bikes and in-line skates. There are four locations along the lakefront (800/915-BIKE).

FESTIVALS

A summerlong round of free festivals includes gospel, blues, jazz and Latin-American music. Taste of Chicago, the Venetian night boat parade and the Chicago Air & Water Show please crowds year after year (312/744-3370).

BASEBALL

Chicago Cubs, 1060 W. Addison St. (773/404-CUBS). Chicago White Sox, 333 W. 35th St. (312/674-1000).

TOURS

The Loop Tour Train—See downtown buildings up close from the El (on Saturday afternoons, June-October). Pick up free tickets in advance at the Chicago Cultural Center (312/744-2400). Chicago Neighborhood Tours—Saturday morning bus trips introduce visitors to the heritage and culture of some of the city's 77 neighborhoods. Ticket charge (312/742-1190). Chicago Architecture Foundation—Join one of more than 60 tours of the city and suburbs with trained docents. Selected tour titles: Early Skyscra-

pers, Modern & Beyond and Architecture River Cruise (312/922-3432).

SHOPPING

State Street—Stores include Marshall Field's, Carson Pirie Scott, Filene's Basement and Toys R Us. Field's has its own visitors center and a concierge service (312/781-4483; store 312/781-1000). North Michigan Avenue — Bloomingdale's, Gucci and Henri Bendel are in the six-story 900 North Michigan Shops. Chicago Place showcases Saks Fifth Avenue, Talbots, Louis Vuitton and Ann Taylor. Water Tower Place anchors are Field's and Lord & Taylor. Freestanding stores include Neiman Marcus, Crate & Barrel, Sony Gallery and Viacom. F.A.O. Schwarz, toy store extraordinaire, is at 840 N. Michigan Ave. (312/587-5000). Nike Town, 669 N. Michigan Ave., combines show biz with everything you need for the sporting life (312/642-6363). Oak Street—Giorgio Armani, Jil Sander and Versace are some of the names you'll see on high-fashion shops along this pretty street just off Michigan Avenue.

NORTH OF CHICAGO

A relaxing drive north on Sheridan Road through a wooded setting by the

lake takes you into the North Shore suburbs with their kid-friendly parks, stately homes and quaint shopping districts. Chicago Botanic Garden—This garden of gardens includes roses, waterfalls, English and Japanese styles, native Illinois prairies, fruits and vegetables on 385 acres. Charge for parking includes admission. Tram tours, additional charge. 1000 Lake Cook Rd., Glencoe (847/835-5440). Ravinia Music Festival— This is the leafy summer home of the Chicago Symphony Orchestra and one of the country's finest outdoor music festivals. Pack a picnic or eat at an on-site restaurant. 400 Iris Ln., Highland Park (847/266-5100).

WEST OF CHICAGO

Frank Lloyd Wright lived and worked for 20 years in the Village of Oak Park. For guided and self-guided walking tours among his Prairie-style buildings, as well as work by other notable architects, contact: Oak Park Visitors Center. Information about Ernest Hemingway sites and other historic house museums and special events is available at the center, 158 N. Forest Ave., Oak Park (708/848-1500).

By Joanne Prim Shade

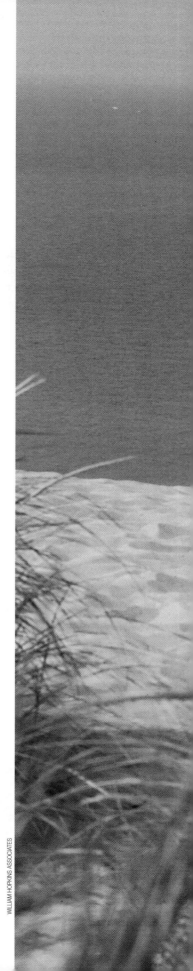

INDIANA'S DUNE COUNTRY

Towering sand dunes crown a stunning landscape of beaches and bogs, prairies and forests.

Massive Ice Age glaciers rumbled across northwestern Indiana 10,000 years ago, then receded, carving a giant bowl at the southern tip of Lake Michigan. The lake marked the glacier's retreat in dramatic fashion, laying down 45 miles of sandy shoreline, the longest such stretch to be found along the entire perimeter of the lake.

Native Americans and French voyageurs first trekked through this area via the Old Calumet Trail (now US-12). In the 1800s, homesteaders laid claim to rich farmland south of the lake, and the towns of LaPorte and Chesterton were born. Steel mills and railroad factories sprang up along the shoreline, drawing waves of immigrants to Gary and Michigan City.

Industry and leisure continue to share the Indiana shoreline, as they have for a century. In the 1920s, as steel mills staked out prime lakeside sites, 50 splashy posters proclaiming "25 miles of beach" were commissioned by the South Shore Line railroad, enticing Chicagoans to visit Indiana's Dunes area, just 50 miles to the southeast. More than 70 years later, the South Shore, the nation's last electric interurban line, still makes daily runs between Chicago's Randolph Street Station and South Bend, Indiana, dropping off Dunes-bound passengers along the way.

Closeup on the Dunes

On summer weekends, I-80/90 and I-94, the main east-west routes through northern Indiana, take a steady stream of visitors to the Dunes. Some head right to the beach; others prowl the antiques shops, galleries and quaint cafes of nearby towns.

The centerpiece of the region, the 15,000-acre Indiana Dunes National Lakeshore, beckons nature lovers, birdwatchers, anglers and water enthusiasts. Standing atop softly sculpted mounds of silvery white sand, you can look northwest across the deep blue waters of Lake Michigan to the building-block outline of downtown Chicago.

Botanists marvel at the diversity of the dunes, where prairie, marsh and forest entwine, and Arctic-region bearberry grows only steps away from desert-friendly prickly pear cactus. The lakeshore ranks fourth among

WILLIAM HOPKINS ASSOCIATES

Midwest Living **readers voted Indiana Dunes State Park their favorite beach.**

national parks in the variety of native plants that it supports. One of the more unusual sites in the national lakeshore is Pinhook Bog, 12 miles south of the lake along State-421. Visitors follow a wood boardwalk to observe the bog's lush population of orchids, tamarack trees, pitcher plants and other carnivorous species.

At the eastern end of the national lakeshore, the tallest active dune, Mt. Baldy, looms 120 feet. Barefoot hikers scurry up the slippery slope on all fours in the early morning hours, before the summer sun sizzles the giant mound of sand. Below, hikers trek miles of beach or follow the more than half-dozen trails that skirt dunes, marshes, bogs and patches of wet prairie. The 9-mile Calumet Trail serves bikers and hikers from the Dune Acres South Shore Line station, east to the Porter-LaPorte county line, a short walk to Mt. Baldy.

Nature is still shaping the lakeshore. Mt. Baldy advances inland about 4 to 5 feet a year. Inland, a thin veneer of soil and vegetation covers older dunes. Closer to the water's edge, "living" dunes shift and grow.

In September, the sky fills with the sound of beating wings and shrill cries, as thousands of migrating loons, geese, ducks and shorebirds pass through the area.

Michigan City

East of the National Lakeshore, Indiana's only lighthouse stands sentinel over the harbor in Michigan City (population: 34,000), as it has for more than a century. Picnickers spread blankets on the shady lawn at Washington Park, a picturesque 90-acre lakefront park with an observation tower and a zoo.

In the days when this hardworking factory town ranked as one of the busiest ports on the Great Lakes, its lighthouse guided freighters riding low under loads of lumber. In the Old Lighthouse Museum, visitors can see exhibits that tell the stories of tragic shipwrecks and room settings showing how lighthouse keepers lived.

Nearby, shops and restaurants fill the renovated Pullman Railroad Car Manufacturing Company building, now called The Works. Throughout, memorabilia and sepia-toned photos chronicling the era when the factory built railroad passenger cars line the building's brick walls. The Works is part of Lighthouse Place, a sprawling outlet mall of mostly upscale stores in the rail yards that once surrounded the factory.

A new generation of Michigan City residents has reclaimed the grand mansions built by prosperous 19th-century industrialists. Guests can overnight at the

Not far from Chicago, a secluded Indiana Dunes beach.

PORTER COUNTY CONVENTION, RECREATION & VISITOR COMMISSION

LA PORTE COUNTY CONVENTION & VISITORS BUREAU

Washington Park in Michigan City, Indiana.

Hutchinson Mansion Inn, where opulent woodwork gleams again and a soaring staircase leads to airy bedrooms.

A 1960s initiative that stocked Lake Michigan with salmon and trout from the American Northwest has paid off handsomely. Michigan City now calls itself the "Coho capital of the Midwest," and charter boats filled with proud anglers boast record catches of coho, Chinook salmon and trout.

Countryside Pleasures

Away from the lakeshore, the terrain rolls gently, then levels, revealing a patchwork of orchards and corn fields. Farmers and fruit growers harvest bushels of berries, peaches, apples and vegetables. On Saturdays during summer and fall, farmers markets in Michigan City and southeast in nearby LaPorte (population: 23,000) are piled high with produce and baked goods.

French fur traders who arrived here in the 1600s gave LaPorte its name. A natural opening in the forest served as a gateway to the prairie land beyond, and

they called it "la porte" (the door). Today, the distinctive octagonal red Door Prairie barn along US-35 south of town welcomes visitors to the area.

West of LaPorte, in Chesterton (population: 9,124), the business district angles around a city park crowned by a charming wooden gazebo. More than two dozen antiques and craft shops have taken over storefronts lining the surrounding streets. In the pink cottage that houses Emma's Antiques, dried flowers scent the air, and cheery blue-and-white vintage china fills cupboards. At Station House Pottery, practical crocks and bowls by more than 60 artists share shelves with graceful pitchers.

Chesterton's visitors have discovered Gray Goose Inn, a rambling bed and breakfast overlooking a lake just north of downtown. Guests pull up to the breakfast table to watch the flocks of geese that frequent the lake and inspired the inn's name. "Our only rule is: Relax and enjoy yourself," innkeeper Chuck Ramsey says. "That's what Dunes-country weekends are all about."

Planning Your Visit to the Indiana Dunes Area

Indiana Dunes country stretches east and west across three lakefront counties. Travelers can take I-80/90, I-94 or US-12, a scenic drive through inland communities and the Indiana Dunes National Lakeshore.

For more information, contact: Indiana Dunes National Lakeshore (219/926-7561, ext. 225); Indiana Department of Commerce, Tourism Development Division (800/289-6646; 317/232-8860). For information about specific areas, call these local convention and visitors bureaus: Lake County (800/ALL-LAKE); LaPorte County (800/634-2650); Porter County (800/283-TOUR). For train service information, contact: South Shore Line (800/356-2079).

LODGINGS

Along with motel chains, lodgings include:

Creekwood Inn—This English manor nestled in 33 acres of woods in Michigan City offers 12 guest rooms and dining at the inn's American Grill. Doubles from $123 (219/872-8357).

The Hutchinson Mansion Inn—Spend the night in lumber baron William Hutchinson's imposing Queen Anne brick mansion in one of Michigan City's historic districts. Doubles from $85 (219/879-1700).

Gray Goose Inn—Eight guest rooms comprise this cozy Chesterton bed and breakfast. Doubles from $80 (800/521-5127).

Indian Oak Resort & Spa—One hundred spacious rooms overlook a private lake and woods near Chesterton. The resort boasts spa packages, walking and cycling trails and an indoor fitness room with 50-foot lap pool. Doubles from $70 (219/926-2200; 800/552-4232).

DINING

Pumps on 12—An original roadhouse about a mile west of Michigan City along US-12 features '50s-style decor, plus burgers, steaks and seafood (219/874-6201).

Wingfield's Restaurant and Irish Pub—Lake perch is a specialty at this lively eatery adjacent to Chesterton's Indian Oak Resort & Spa. It features Irish entertainment and a comedy club every week (219/926-2200).

Port Drive-In—You don't have to get out of your car to enjoy a frosty mug of the Port's brewed-right-here root beer. At this old-time Chesterton eatery, car hops come to you to take your order for beverages, burgers, fries and onion rings (219/926-3500).

Roskoe's—Enjoy sunset views from the sprawling deck at this dockside restaurant on Pine Lake, one of the three small lakes within LaPorte city limits (219/325-3880).

ANTIQUES & SHOPPING

Lighthouse Place Outlet Center, Michigan City—See pages 66-67 (219/879-6506).

The Antique Market—Browse a wide range of antiques and collectibles in Michigan City (219/879-4084).

Coachman Antique Mall in LaPorte—See this 80-dealer mall, then pick up a brochure with directions to 15 more area antiques shops (219/326-5933).

Prairie Farm Antiques—This 1860s barn in tiny Rolling Prairie is chock-full of vintage goodies (219/778-2892).

Quail Ridge Farm—In LaPorte, themed gardens display perennials and herbs; a gift shop sells garden accessories and books (219/778-2194).

The Chesterton Art Gallery—Pottery, paintings, sculpture and other works, many depicting Dunes themes, by more than 200 artists are shown at this combination gallery and studio art instruction program in Chesterton (219/926-4711).

The Yellow Brick Road Gift Shop & Fantasy Museum—Shop for *Wizard of Oz* collector items, dollhouse kits, dolls and Victorian ornaments. The Fantasy Museum's mementos, photos and exhibits recall scenes from the famous tale (219/926-7048).

Station House Pottery—See page 67 for details (219/926-7781).

Emma's Antiques—See page 67 for details about this Chesterton shop (219/929-4427).

National Lakeshore and offers swimming, fishing (for smelt only), access to the Calumet Trail for walking and biking, and a nature center (219/926-1952).

Red Arrow Ventures, Ltd.—A complete horseback riding and trail-riding facility with 4 miles of trails that wind through woods north of Michigan City (219/872-2114).

Royal Acres Equestrian Center—Set on 46 acres, this technologically advanced facility specializes in English riding lessons in Michigan City (219/874-7519).

(219/921-0380); Allen Bigelow Cheers Sailboat Charters, Michigan City (312/315-2345); CMS Marine (powerboat rentals), Portage (219/763-7308).

Golf—Hit the links at the Course at Aberdeen, Aberdeen (see page 71) (219/462-5050); Duck Creek Country Club, Hobart (219/759-2674); Briar Leaf Golf Club, LaPorte (219/326-1992); Sand Creek Country Club, Chesterton (219/395-5210).

FARMERS MARKETS, ORCHARDS & PRODUCE

Farms and orchards dot the countryside around LaPorte and Michigan City. The LaPorte County Fruit & Vegetable Growers Association publishes a helpful map showing roughly 30 fruit growers, "U-pick" roadside stands and vegetable markets in the county (219/326-6808).

Michigan City Mainstreet Farmers Market—Shop on Saturday mornings, May-October (800/634-2650).

LaPorte Farmers Market—Stop by on Saturday mornings, May-October (800/634-2650).

Enjoy fresh breezes and smooth sailing along Indiana Dunes National Lakeshore.

PORTER COUNTY CONVENTION, RECREATION & VISITOR COMMISSION

PARKS & RECREATION

Indiana Dunes National Lakeshore—See pages 64-66. Trail maps and information are available at the visitors center along US-12 (219/926-7561).

Indiana Dunes State Park—With 3 miles of shoreline, the state-run park is situated in the center of Indiana Dunes

Charter Fishing—For information, contact the county convention and visitors bureaus (see page 68) or North Coast Charter Association (219/845-5993).

Boating—Choose a charter: Amazing Grace Yacht Charters, Portage (219/764-2852); American Yacht Charters, Michigan City

AREA ATTRACTIONS

Old Lighthouse Museum—Rare Fresnell lenses are on display in Michigan City. Open 1 to 4 p.m., Tuesdays-

Sundays. Adults $2 (219/872-6133).

Washington Park and Washington Park Zoo— The hours of this zoo in Michigan City vary by season, March—December (219/873-1510).

Bailly Homestead/ Chellberg Farm—Tour the home of Porter County's first white settler, French-Canadian voyageur and fur trader Joseph Bailly, and a turn-of-the-century 80-acre working farm established by Swedish immigrants.

Indiana Dunes National Lakeshore—Near Porter, it's open daily and it's free (219/926-7561, ext. 225).

Barker Mansion—Formal gardens surround a 38-room 1857 English manor-style mansion furnished with original art, lovely marble and exquisite woodwork. Open year-round, admission is $3 for adults (219/873-1520).

Door Prairie Auto Museum—Three floors showcase a century of classic cars, airplanes, antique toys and re-created storefront facades from three eras in LaPorte. Open April to December, $5 for adults (219/326-1337).

Hesston Steam Museum— Operating steam equipment is shown outdoors in Hesston. Steam-train rides traverse 155 acres. The museum is open noon to 5 p.m. on week-

ends, Memorial Day-Labor Day; Sundays only in October (219/872-7405).

World's Fair Homes— Self-guided auto tour takes in five unique homes designed for the 1933 Chicago World's Fair Century of Progress Exhibition, then brought by barge to the lakeside community of Beverly Shores. Pick up a guide at the visitors center, Indiana Dunes National Lakeshore along

Fall brings families out to the Bailly Homestead for the Duneland Harvest Festival, a look at life in the 1800s.

US-12 (219/926-7561 ext. 225).

Porcelain-Enameled All-Steel Streamlined Historic Home— Designed in the 1940s, this Lustron home in Chesterton is among fewer than 2,500 such houses nationwide. It features 1930s Norman Bel Geddes furnishings. The tour is free, but open only by appointment (219/926-3669).

SHOPPING

Save the Dunes Gift Shop—This shop along

US-12 just west of Beverly Shores in Michigan City is operated by the Save the Dunes Council. It is filled with nature photography, art prints, paintings, books, posters and jewelry (219/879-3937).

Dune Antiques and Interiors—Custom-painted furniture, rustic hickory chairs and cabin- and lodge-style furnishings fill this shop in the lakeside town of Beverly Shores (219/879-2368).

Prairie Farm Antiques— This 1860s barn in the tiny farming community of Rolling Prairie sells antique glassware, clocks, furniture and more (219/778-2892).

FESTIVALS

Lakefront Art Festival— Midwest artists display their wares at Washington Park along the lakefront in Michigan City on the third weekend in August

PORTER COUNTY CONVENTION, RECREATION & VISITOR COMMISSION

(219/872-5055; 800/634-2650). Lakefront Music Festival—Take in musical performances from bluegrass to classical in July along the lakefront in Michigan City's Washington Park. Chesterton Art and Crafts Fair—For more than 40 years, the first weekend in August has brought together more than 100 potters, weavers, painters and regional artists for a 2-day open-air art fair sponsored by The Chesterton Art Gallery (219/926-4711).

OTHER PLACES TO VISIT IN THE AREA

Miller Beach, Gary

Reach the sheltered lakefront community of Miller Beach by taking I-80/90 west to the US-6 exit south then traveling west on US-12 to Lake Street, which heads north to the beach. Originally a fishing and ice-harvesting center, Miller Beach became a town in 1907 and later was annexed by Gary.

The 270-acre Marquette Park includes 3 miles of shoreline and dunes. A marker in the park commemorates Gustave Chanute's history-making glider flights over Miller Dunes in 1896. The park's bathhouse and twin-towered pavilion and columned front entrance are examples of Prairie School architecture. Off the beach along Lake Street and Miller Avenue are galleries, shops and restaurants.

Worth a stop is the Miller Bakery Cafe, a contemporary bistro known for inventive cuisine such as spring lamb shank with root vegetables and herbs, and asparagus salad tossed with sesame rice vinegar dressing (219/938-2229).

Locals also like Customs/Mambo for browsing through an assortment of terra-cotta wares, then grabbing a bite of Mexican food in the courtyard eatery (219/939-1933). Contact: Lake County Convention & Visitors Bureau (219/980-1617; 800/ALL-LAKE).

Valparaiso

Ten miles south of Lake Michigan off US-30, Valparaiso's name comes from the old Chilean seaport of Valparaiso, where Commodore Porter (the county's namesake) led a naval battle. The parklike campus of Valparaiso University anchors this town of 25,000. The college's stunning Chapel of the Resurrection with soaring stained-glass windows ranks as the world's largest college chapel. A stroll around the downtown square passes the castlelike Old Jail Museum built in 1871. At the 1893 Memorial Opera House, stenciling, stained glass and sparkling chandeliers rekindle the opulent feel of the Victorian era. A century-old downtown livery stable with brick walls, beamed ceiling and plank floors houses LIFESTYLES: the Gallery. The shop displays original art, photographs, sculpture, glass and drawings (219/464-9167). Collectors will want to find their way to Valparaiso Antiques, two floors of furniture, glass, jewelry and primitives (219/465-1869).

The comfortable Inn at Aberdeen is a handsome Queen Anne-style 1890s home and gardens renovated to house 11 luxurious guest rooms with balconies and fireplaces. Doubles from $90 (219/465-3753).

Dining options include the Strongbow Inn, where roast turkey with all the trimmings is daily fare (219/462-5121). At Restaurante Don Quixote, sample paella (saffron rice with fresh shellfish) and other Spanish specialties (219/462-7976). Contact: Valparaiso Chamber of Commerce (219/462-1105).

By Peggy Ammerman

LAKE MICHIGAN'S EAST SHORE

Midwesterners first recognized the special vacation magic of Lake Michigan's east shore more than a century ago, swapping steamy summertime Detroit and Chicago for woodsy hideaways and waterside retreats.

Western Michigan welcomes visitors with spectacular sunsets and a climate that fosters fruit trees and blesses vineyards from Harbor Country to Traverse Bay. Salmon thrive in the lake waters, and trout populate nearby rivers.

Dunes and lighthouses share the shoreline, providing endless photo opportunities. Expansive national and state forests parallel Lake Michigan, with biking and hiking trails inviting exploration. You can book a cruise at an up-to-date marina or wander wharves lined with shops, galleries and cafes. For an overnight stay, choose from fanciful bed and breakfasts, plain-and-simple cottages, primitive campgrounds or posh resorts.

Saugatuck's summer art school and Interlochen's famed music camp hint at the cultural pursuits here. Union Pier and Lakeside lure antiques buffs. And the legacy of Michigan's 19th-century timber industry is on view in the grand commercial buildings and elegant lumber-baron mansions of Manistee and Ludington.

The places and events we tell you about here will get you off to a good start. You're sure to discover dozens more as you roam Lake Michigan's east shore.

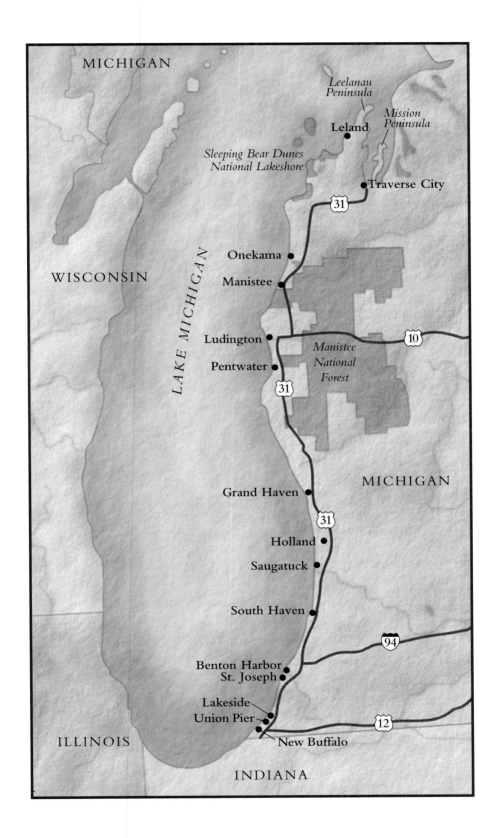

MICHIGAN

Leelanau Peninsula

Mission Peninsula

Leland

Sleeping Bear Dunes National Lakeshore

Traverse City

31

WISCONSIN

LAKE MICHIGAN

Onekama

Manistee

Ludington

10

Pentwater

Manistee National Forest

31

MICHIGAN

Grand Haven

31

Holland

Saugatuck

South Haven

94

Benton Harbor
St. Joseph

Lakeside
Union Pier

12

New Buffalo

ILLINOIS

INDIANA

MICHIGAN'S HARBOR COUNTRY

A string of old-time vacation towns blend sophistication and laid-back charm.

Even before US-12 (the road that curves around the base of Lake Michigan) was paved in the 1920s, carloads of Chicagoans happily cranked up their Model T's for the bone-jolting 70-mile trip that took them to the lush fruit orchards and plentiful fishing waiting in southwestern Michigan, just past the Indiana border. Soon modest vacation homes and cottages were nestling along the white sand beaches and amid woodsy countryside of New Buffalo, Union Pier, Lakeside, Harbert and Three Oaks.

By the 1950s, though, Harbor Country was considered ho-hum. The tiny towns strung along the lakeshore languished like a strand of heirloom pearls tucked away in a keepsake chest. Chicagoans rediscovered their luster in the 1980s. Ninety minutes away from the gritty city, on the other side of the lake, the waters were warmer, the breezes were cooler and the good life was waiting. Now *Chicago* magazine calls Harbor Country "the hottest weekend-escape territory in the Midwest."

Up the Coast to New Buffalo

The towns of Harbor Country meander along US-12 and the Red Arrow Highway, communities of bed and breakfasts, art galleries, antiques shops and stylish cafes, all with an appealing low-key ambience. Local history holds that the area's first paying guests showed up in 1870. A Lakeside farmer hosted them, charging $7 a week for all the swimming, hiking and picnicking the visitors could handle.

A quarter-century later, passenger trains from Chicago chugged through Harbor Country, dropping off vacationers all along the way from New Buffalo to South Haven, 50 miles north. In 1922, the railroad built a hotel and a giant roundhouse in New Buffalo. It has been preserved and now houses shops and businesses. Next door, in a replica of the original depot, the New Buffalo Railroad Museum displays a meticulously crafted model train layout depicting the town at the turn of the century. Also in the depot is the Harbor Country Chamber of Commerce, the place to go for

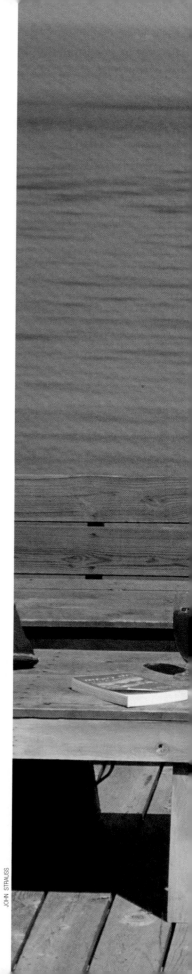

JOHN STRAUSS

Near Union Pier, the Pine Garth Inn's deck overlooks a private beach.

visitor information about the area.

New Buffalo, dubbed the "Gateway to Michigan," is Harbor Country's largest town, with a population of 2,300. Michigan's first tourist information center opened here in 1934. Its successor, the modern New Buffalo Welcome Center off I-94 at exit 1, 1 mile north of the Indiana state line, is Michigan's busiest.

This temperate stretch of Lake Michigan shoreline is a favorite of anglers and boaters. Legend has it that in a single day in 1872, a fishing boat here netted 16,000 pounds of whitefish. Chinook salmon and feisty steelhead trout are among the trophy-size catches anglers vie for today.

From New Buffalo north to Mackinac Island at the top of the state, boaters will find a marina every 15 miles. New Buffalo's marina is known as one of the best along Lake Michigan's eastern shore, and days dawn to a bustling scene quayside. By late morning, sailboats are slowly motoring into slips and docking for the day.

Sailors so inclined can trade their sea legs to browse the more than two dozen shops along a two-block stretch of Whittaker Street, reaching inland from the harbor. There are paintings at the Silver Crane Gallery, rustic twig furniture and peeled-log headboards at Hearthwoods, and cookware and clothing at The Shops at Michigan Thyme, a row of storefronts

shaded by dark green canvas awnings. Lunchtime finds the courtyards tucked behind turn-of-the-century storefront restaurants brimming with diners.

Union Pier and Lakeside

You may find it hard to keep your eyes on the road as you travel north from New Buffalo along the old tree-lined four-lane that links the Harbor Country towns. It's the Red Arrow Highway, named after a Michigan World War I Army division. Beckoning from both sides of the road are vintage roadhouses and summer cottages, now transformed into art galleries or antiques shops, bed and breakfasts or casual restaurants with savvy chefs at work in the kitchens.

In Union Pier, a white frame 1920s resort and dance hall flourishes as Miller's Country House. In the grill room, diners can choose a table overlooking the woodland garden or watch chefs prepare rack of lamb or barbecue ribs in the exhibition kitchen. Next door, The Wine Sellers, Inc., is an intimately scaled shop stocking local wines and those from small estates and family-owned vineyards elsewhere.

Just up the road from Union Pier lies the town of Lakeside, once called Clay Banks, for the 80-foot bluff that long ago

Gift and antiques shops thrive in Harbor Country.

JOHN STRAUSS

Head to St. Joseph's North Pier to fish or just admire the lighthouse.

JOHN STRAUSS

served as a sailors' landmark. By the 1920s, at the height of Lakeside's popularity, a dozen resorts dotted the town's south side.

One of these, the sprawling three-story Lakeside Inn, was renovated and reopened as a 30-room inn. Vintage porcelain sinks lend charm to guest rooms. Wicker chairs, Arts and Crafts-era antiques and a rustic see-through fireplace in the lobby evoke a classic vacation-lodge feeling. In the morning, guests on their way to breakfast on the enclosed back porch slip through a quaint ballroom lined with animal trophies and historic photos of Native Americans. Rockers lining the 100-foot front porch provide prime seating for sunset views.

Harbor Country Treats

Harbor Country once had a good-sized Swedish-American community, including Heartland poet Carl Sandburg, who owned a summer home in Harbert. It's a good bet he grew up enjoying some of the same treats you can find at the Harbert Swedish Bakery. It's known for its Swedish limpa bread, hazelnut butter cookies and ginger molasses cookies. Come early—by 2 p.m. on weekends, the shelves are bare.

At Heart of the Vineyard, on a farm 9 miles east of Bridgman, wine lovers sip Harvest Delight, a late-season honey-and-apricot-flavored white wine. A few yards away, a reconstructed round barn from Fulton County, Indiana, houses a cognac-making operation.

With late summer comes the bounty of the fruit harvest. Visitors delay their antiquing and fishing and head to rural orchards and canopied roadside stands to taste the flavor of Harbor Country captured in ripe, luscious peaches.

Planning Your Visit to Harbor Country

For visitor information about the area stretching from the Indiana state line north to Sawyer, contact: Harbor Country Chamber of Commerce (616/469-5409). For information about the entire southwestern Michigan region, contact: Southwestern Michigan Tourist Council (616/925-6301).

LODGINGS

The Harbor Country Lodging Association has a 24-hour phone line (800/362-7251). Lodging choices include bed and breakfasts, inns, condominium and cottage rentals, and newer hotels and motels.

Bauhaus on Barton— This renovated 1948 home in a tree-lined New Buffalo neighborhood is furnished with blond 1950s furniture, chenille bedspreads, vintage lamps and accessories. Doubles from $95 (616/469-6419).

The Harbor Grand Hotel & Suites—Alongside New Buffalo's marina, this newer four-story hotel has harbor views and easy access to nearby shops and dining. Doubles from $170 (616/469-7700).

Inn at Union Pier— Called the Hotel Karonsky in the 1920s, the resort comprises 16 rooms in three buildings roughly 200 feet from the beach. Rooms in The Great House and The Pier House feature antique Swedish ceramic fireplaces. Doubles from $145. The Cottage of the Four Seasons has four rooms. Doubles from $125 (616/469-4700).

Pine Garth Inn—Now a bed and breakfast, this one-time posh summer home in Union Pier has lake views from every room. Doubles from $120 (616/469-1642).

The Gordon Beach Inn— This historic lakefront inn in Lakeside was built in the 1920s. Recently renovated, it pleases guests with hand-stenciled walls in Native American and botanical themes. Doubles from $75 (616/469-0800).

Lakeside Inn—A lobby fireplace and a broad front porch give this 30-room inn in Lakeside a homey lodge look. Carefully chosen antiques add a refined note. Doubles from $75 (616/469-0600).

The Pebble House— Known nationally for its rich collection of Arts and Crafts furnishings and stained-glass lamps, the seven rooms and suites of this Lakeside bed and breakfast are in three buildings connected by walkways. The breakfast buffet includes home-baked specialties and egg dishes. Doubles from $95 (616/469-1416).

Beachwalk Rental— Luxury beach homes are available weekly in Michigan City, Indiana, 10 miles south of New Buffalo. Memorial Day to Labor Day, from $500 to $2,700 per week (800/814-7501; 219/879-7874). Other vacation rentals include: Kate Frankel Rentals (summer, 616/469-5719; winter, 773/935-7742); The Leasing Company (616/469-5573); Cottages for Rent, Inc. (800/471-6936).

DINING

Oink's Dutch Treat— This pink and turquoise ice cream shop along US-12 in New Buffalo is a local landmark, attracting throngs on summer afternoons. While ice cream lovers wait in line for creamy lemon custard and 55 other flavors, they pore over owner Roger Vink's collection of vintage ice cream dippers and dairy memorabilia lining the walls (616/469-3535).

Mariner's Cove—This rambling wood-frame eatery across from the New Buffalo marina offers a postcard-perfect view of the harbor. At dusk, diners gravitate to the outdoor patio and watch the sunset from the hull of the landlocked vessel SS Minnow, now a bar (616/469-5323).

Miller's Country House— This casual fine dining spot on popular Union Pier creatively prepares seafood and a wide choice of grilled meats. It's open for lunch and dinner daily in season (616/469-5950).

The Casual Chef Cafe— At this eatery along the Red Arrow Highway, vegetarian chili and thick turkey breast sandwiches are always on the lunch menu. Drop in for breakfast

salsas. The restaurant closes on Tuesdays (616/756-6002).

Heyerdall's—A Red Arrow Highway fixture since 1927, this roomy roadhouse cafe serves home-style stewed chicken dinners and a Swedish plate with potato, pork and veal sausages, and brown beans in a spicy, sweet sauce (616/465-5546).

Jenny's Restaurant— In Lakeside, an intimate, candlelit dining room creates a relaxed setting for favorite dishes such as Thai Chilean sea bass

Tosi's and Tosi's Cafe— In Stevensville, the original Tosi's features authentic northern Italian cuisine with homemade pasta and Asiago cheese bread. Tosi's Cafe in downtown St. Joseph combines Italian fare with lighter dishes (616/429-3689).

Harbert Swedish Bakery—This is a favorite stop along the Red Arrow Highway in Harbert for authentic Scandinavian-style baked goodies (616/469-1777).

SHOPS, ANTIQUES & GALLERIES

Hearthwoods—Owner Andrew Brown uses native pine and oak to fashion rustic twig furniture and peeled-log headboards in New Buffalo (616/469-5572).

Michigan Thyme, Ltd. and The Cafe at Michigan Thyme— Gourmet foods, kitchen ware and a cafe fill one side of this New Buffalo shop; sundresses in splashy prints and hand-painted clothing hang at the other (616/469-3470).

The Silver Crane Gallery—Featured here are jewelry and limited-edition prints with a southwest flavor plus the works of local artist Carol Shabbaz. Gallery owner and former Chicagoan Herb Crane explains New Buffalo's allure: "We're close to

THE PEBBLE HOUSE

BED & BREAKFAST INN

15093 LAKESHORE RD.

Ed and Jean Lawrence's inn, The Pebble House, takes its name from the Lake Michigan stones on its exterior.

GUY HURKA

and dinner, too (616/469-1200).

Froehlich's—Cyclists head to this quaint storefront cafe and bakery in Three Oaks for takeout and eat-in soups, spicy salami and marinated vegetables piled on whole grain baguettes, side salads, cookies, muffins and homemade jams and

with steamed rice and pecan-laden chocolate pie (616/469-6545).

Tabor Hill Winery—This establishment overlooks Tabor Hill Vineyards in Buchanan. The creative menu includes Norwegian salmon wrapped in grape leaves, fresh crab cakes and Raspberry Chicken (800/283-3363).

the city, but it feels a million miles away" (616/469-4000).

Art Barn Gallery North—Find pottery, jewelry, wearable art and paintings of dunes and lakeshore scenes are found at this New Buffalo gallery and teaching art center (616/469-5550).

Twelve Cedars Vintage Furniture—This Union Pier store sells antique European furniture (616/469-0304).

Fenway Gallery—A white frame house in Lakeside showcases works by the owners, Bruce Wood and William Janosco, plus glass, paintings and furniture by more than 25 artists (616/469-2818).

Lakeside Antiques—A spacious barn holds 1930s metal porch furniture, blond 1940s Heywood Wakefield chests and tables, and advertising signs. Quirky finds lurk around every corner (616/469-4467).

Rabbit Run Art & Antiques—Antiques in attractive room settings bring browsers to this Lakeside shop (616/857-5174).

The Weekend Weaver—This Bridgman store offers weaving supplies and a selection of hand-loomed crafts by local artists (616/465-3455).

FESTIVALS

Apple Cider Century Bike Tour—Thousands attend this 20-year-old event in Three Oaks the last Sunday in September. It's one of the largest bicycle tours in the U.S. (616/756-3361).

Ice Cream Social—Family fun and ice cream are dished up in early August at Lakeside Park, an annual tradition since the 1920s (616/469-5409).

Lakeside Arts & Crafts Festival—Midwest artisans and crafters sell paintings, pottery, jewelry and handwoven textiles during early July (616/469-5409).

Ship and Shore Festival—

Harbor Country fun includes hang-gliding from Tower Hill in Warren Dunes State Park, near Sawyer.

Don't miss the grand boat parade, music, food, games and a fireworks display the first weekend in August (616/469-5409).

SIGHTSEEING & RECREATION

New Buffalo Railroad Museum—Marvel at the collection of railroad memorabilia and a model train layout showing the town in the early 1900s (616/469-5409).

Warren Dunes State Park—Near Sawyer, sand hills soar to heights of 240 feet along a broad, 2½-mile-long beach. Campsites with electrical hookups are available (800/44-PARKS).

Warren Woods State Park—Like the state park listed above, this park is named for local conservationist E. K. Warren, who made a fortune in the last century manufacturing corset stays from turkey feathers. Follow the trails along the Gallien River to see abundant wildflowers in this primeval forest west of Three Oaks (616/426-4013).

New Buffalo Municipal Marina—Dock boats at the foot of New Buffalo's Whittaker Street (616/469-6887).

New Buffalo Beach and Weko Beach, Bridgman—These two towns have well-maintained public beaches with cold outdoor showers, boat launches and concessions (616/469-5409). Three Oaks Spokes Bicycle Museum and Information Center— Stop by the red brick train depot to pick up cycling route maps and to see the display of historic and unusual bicycles (616/756-3361).

FRUIT STANDS & VINEYARDS

Along the highway and in towns throughout the area, fruit growers and vegetable farmers stock produce stands all summer long. Contact: Southwestern Michigan Tourist Council (616/925-6301) for a copy of "Pick Michigan," a guide listing farmers markets, orchards, vineyards and festivals. Tabor Hill Winery and Restaurant; Tabor Hill Champagne Cellar—In Buchanan, visit this combination winery and gourmet restaurant (800/283-3363). The Champagne Cellar in Bridgman features a tasting room stocked with premium wines, food products and juices (800/283-3363). St. Julian Wine Company—Michigan's oldest winery has six locations, with a tasting room in Union Pier (616/469-3150). Heart of the Vineyard Winery and Tasting Center—The Winery

nestles in the hills 5 miles east of Bridgman on a 30-acre farm. Look for the Tasting Center along the Red Arrow Highway just north of Union Pier (800/716-9463).

OTHER PLACES TO VISIT IN THE AREA

St. Joseph

A short 20-mile drive up Lake Michigan's shore from the towns of Harbor Country, the twin cities of St. Joseph and Benton Harbor straddle the mouth of the St. Joseph River. Tourist-oriented St. Joseph has a population of 10,000 and hard-working Benton Harbor, 15,000. Folks 100 years ago flocked to St. Joseph to sip its mineral waters. The bluff-top city's vintage downtown boasts brick-paved streets, inviting benches, period lighting and baskets of flowers.

Nearby, monuments and the historic Maids of the Mist fountain dot a mile-long city park. From the park, steps lead to Lake Michigan below. Here, Silver Beach offers a beachfront with modern shelters and a playground. Two light-houses jut into the city's harbor, crowning the end of twin 1,000-foot piers.

In July, the Venetian Festival draws crowds with boating events, food and fireworks.

St. Joseph is popular with anglers; several

fishing charter services are based here. Trophy-sized salmon and trout populate the lake; the river yields walleye pike and smallmouth bass. Contact: Cornerstone Chamber Services (616/925-6100).

South Haven

Thirty miles north of St. Joseph, the summer population of picturesque lakeside South Haven swells from 6,000 to around 20,000. Eateries and shops scatter along the harbor at the mouth of the Black River. Tall wood-frame bed and breakfasts, built as inns during the town's tourist boom in the 1880s, line North Shore Drive. Two such houses make up Yelton Manor Bed and Breakfast. Guest rooms feature fireplaces and sumptuous baths (616/637-5220).

Much of Michigan's plentiful blueberry crop comes from the surrounding farm country. South Haven celebrates the National Blueberry Festival each August. Year-round, an assortment of blueberry-themed clothing, gifts and food items fill The Blueberry Store (616/637-6322). Contact: Lakeshore Convention & Visitors Bureau (616/637-5252).

By Peggy Ammerman

SAUGATUCK AND GRAND HAVEN

Vacation pleasures on and off the water abound in these pretty Michigan towns.

Arts-centered Saugatuck and boating-oriented Grand Haven, Michigan, share the undulating ribbon of blue water, golden sands and lush green vegetation that make up the Lake Michigan shoreline. One-third of the way up the western edge of Michigan's Lower Peninsula and separated by only 35 miles, both create a playground geared to outdoor enthusiasts and urban sophisticates.

Saugatuck

This genteel hamlet of 2,000 hugs the east bank of the Kalamazoo River before it curves into Lake Michigan. The area's population swells tenfold in summer, with visitors lured by lapping waves and the rhythmic sweep of sand dunes. Orchards flourish to the east and summer cottages grace the countryside all around.

A group of Chicago artists was among the vacationers who found their way here a century ago. Charmed by the bucolic countryside in 1910, they captured scenic Saugatuck on a broad palette by launching the Summer School of Painting on Ox-Bow Lagoon.

Today, the arts continue to complement Saugatuck's natural allure. The Art Institute of Chicago runs Ox-Bow's summer courses in sculpting, painting, ceramics, photography and other media. More than two dozen galleries dot Saugatuck and neighboring Douglas, just west of the river, earning the area the honorary title of "Art Coast of Michigan." There's more art on view at Ox-Bow at the end of Park Street.

Visitors are amused to find the area so steeped in art that even the public restrooms in harborside Willow Park have benefited. A wall there displays a hand-done reproduction of the pointillist Georges Seurat's familiar *Sunday on Le Grande Jatte.*

Stroll downtown Saugatuck and you won't see just art galleries, but an impressive assortment of clothing, home furnishings and antiques shops as well.

Attractions and activities abound. The popular

JOHN STRAUSS

Galleries and shops
line downtown
Saugatuck streets.

Red Barn Playhouse stages a lively bill of plays and musicals from June through August. The vineyards of western Michigan's wine-making country are nearby. Ask at the visitors bureau for information about tours and tastings.

Lakeside Fun

Visitors engage in a favorite pastime, watching the boat traffic pass through the busy harbor. Powerboats gun their motors, and sailboats glide past stately yachts, some crafted by Saugatuck's own Broward Marine shipbuilders. More than 900 vessels call this port home, inviting admiration from those strolling the piers or the boardwalk that loops around downtown.

Several boats welcome visitors aboard. The paddle wheeler *Star of Saugatuck* and the cruise boat *City of Douglas* ply the waters of the Kalamazoo River and venture onto Lake Michigan. The *Saugatuck Ferry*, North America's only hand-cranked chain ferry, shuttles passengers across the river between downtown Saugatuck and Douglas. The current 24-passenger ferry, built in 1956, is a confection of Victorian arches and gingerbread trim.

Those who prefer swimming to boating head to Oval Beach. The beach ranks among the finest in the country, according to Condé Nast's *Traveler* magazine, MTV and the owners of all those bright umbrellas and striped sling chairs eased back on its golden sands. Dunes thatched with tall breeze-blown grasses rise behind the beach, forming hollows for more private sunning.

Tired of splashing? Roam the dunes in an 18-passenger "schooner." Go out on foot and scale the 279 steps to the top of Mount Baldhead. Or, head over to a very cool place to spend a hot summer afternoon—the Saugatuck Drug Store, where kids and grownups sip frosty cherry phosphates and dip into hand-scooped malts served at an old-fashioned soda fountain.

Grand Haven

Vacation memories of Grand Haven seem to center on the lighted musical fountain downtown. Throngs of eager boaters and pedestrians head to the Grand River's banks at nightfall. There, multicolored illuminated plumes of water dance to rock, classical and other recorded music to

Saugatuck Ferry crosses the Kalamazoo River.

JOHN STRAUSS

Grand Haven's spectacular musical fountain.

JOHN STRAUSS

the delight of spectators.

Grand Haven takes its name from the Grand River, the waterway that passes through the heart of town on its way to Lake Michigan. In the early 1600s, Indian and French trappers canoed its waters; traders established a post on its banks in the late 1700s; and 19th-century loggers filled its rushing waters with forests of pine logs.

A boardwalk traces about 3 miles of the Grand River's south shore, starting at Chinook Pier downtown and ending at the red lighthouse that juts into Lake Michigan. Along the way, the walk meanders past marinas, parks, businesses and a local history museum. With its main street of red brick storefronts and shady broadleaf trees, the town truly is a grand haven for its 13,000 residents and the tens of thousands more who visit the lake and river each summer.

Harborside Pleasures

Before they leave Chinook Pier, anglers ready their boats with ice to chill down the luckless salmon, trout and other sport fish they'll be bringing back. Pedestrians have other fish to fry. They reel in homemade chocolates from Candyland or snag crispy waffle cones packed with Harbor Island fudge ice cream from Temptations sweet shop. On Wednesday evenings, entranced landlubbers watch mainsails and spinnakers billow during the Grand River Sailing Club's weekly races.

Getting acquainted with Grand Haven is easy. The *Harbor Steamer* paddle wheeler takes sightseers on narrated tours of the harbor, Lake Michigan and Spring Lake just to the east. The Harbor Trolley rolls through downtown Grand Haven and Spring Lake, with the driver noting points of interest during 30-minute jaunts.

Cyclists can explore under their own steam on extensive bike paths that traverse the area. The black-topped Lakeshore Path heads south roughly 20 miles to the colorful and quaint Dutch community of Holland.

Planning Your Visit to Saugatuck

For more information, contact: Saugatuck/ Douglas Convention & Visitors Bureau (616/857-1701; fax 616/857-2319; or www.saugatuck.com).

LODGINGS

Saugatuck claims the title of "Bed & Breakfast Capital of the Midwest." Choose from more than 36 bed and breakfasts, several within walking distance of Lake Michigan.

Shady Shore Inn Cottages & Marina—Originally an 1870s shipbuilder's house, the inn brims with period and eclectic furnishings. Some guest rooms have whirlpools and fireplaces. Sixteen seasonal cottages, some with kitchenettes, are available, too. From $65 to $180 (616/857-4387).

Fairchild House—This downtown bed and breakfast with three rooms has feather beds, fine antiques and gourmet breakfasts. Doubles from $125 (616/857-5985).

Ship 'n' Shore Motel—This "boatel" offers 40 units on the Kalamazoo River in downtown Saugatuck. An outdoor heated pool and whirlpool accent the landscaped grounds. Slips available. Doubles from $125 (616/857-2194).

Goshorn Lake Family Resort—Some of the 20 housekeeping cottages have fireplaces; all have fully equipped kitchens. Located 1.5 miles northeast of Saugatuck, it's near a private swimming beach with picnic tables and barbecue grills available. Weekly rates $595 to $1,350 (800/541-4210; 616/857-4808).

CAMPING

To secure a site in advance at a Michigan state park and to inquire about fees, call the central reservation service at 800/44-PARKS (800/447-2757). For other information, contact each park directly.

Allegan State Game Area—No reservations are required for camping at 186 rustic sites (pump water and pit toilets) on three campgrounds 8 miles southeast of Saugatuck. Rates are $6 a night for regular camping; $10 for horseman's campground (616/673-0378). For information about eagle sightings and waterfall activity, contact: Department of Natural Resources, Allegan office (616/673-2430).

DINING

Billies Boathouse—At this local favorite in downtown Saugatuck, savor seafood, steaks, pastas, Mexican entrées and other fare; listen to live music on weekends (616/857-1188).

Chequers—Enjoy a taste of Britain: Wash down fish and chips or shepherd's pie with a stout and finish up with raspberry trifle (616/857-1868).

Kalico Kitchen—Along the Blue Star Memorial Highway in Douglas, try southern-style breakfasts of eggs, biscuits and gravy (616/857-2678).

Belvedere Inn & Restaurant—Grilled quail, tournedos of beef and other haute cuisine are served in dining rooms of a 1913 Georgian-style estate ⅛ mile north of Saugatuck along 63rd St. This stylish inn has 10 elegant guest rooms (616/857-5501).

Crane's Pie Pantry—Locally grown apples, cherries, raspberries and peaches burst from pies and streudels 7 miles from Saugatuck along State-89. Sandwiches and soups round out the menu (616/561-2297).

GALLERIES

You'll count at least 24 galleries here and in neighboring Douglas. See more artwork at Ox-Bow, a summer art school at the end of Park St., open to the public 7:30 p.m. to 10 p.m. on Fridays in the summer. Exhibitions and performances change weekly (616/857-5811).

PERFORMING ARTS

Red Barn Playhouse— This professional summer stock theater 2 miles north of town stages plays and musicals from June through Labor Day (616/857-7707).

SIGHTSEEING

Star of Saugatuck— Take a 1.5-hour cruise on an 82-passenger stern-wheel paddleboat down the Kalamazoo River and, conditions permitting, onto Lake Michigan. Adults pay $8.50, children $5 (616/857-4261).

During Grand Haven's Coast Guard Festival in July, you can tour Coast Guard vessels.

Saugatuck Ferry—Board near Ship 'n' Shore Motel in Saugatuck for a ride across the Kalamazoo River on a 24-passenger vessel pulled by a hand-cranked chain. The ferry operates 9 a.m. to dusk daily Memorial Day-Labor Day. Fare: $1 for adults, 50 cents for kids (no phone). **SS Keewatin Maritime**

Museum—In Douglas, tour the museum and 350-foot steamship, launched in 1907. Adults pay $4.50, kids $2 (616/857-2107). **Saugatuck Dune Rides—** Take a 35-minute tour in an open-air buggy that holds 18 passengers. Adults pay $10.50, $6.50 for children ages 3 to 10 (616/857-2253).

FESTIVALS

In June, the Taste of Saugatuck, held along downtown Water Street, features samplings from local restaurants and an arts-and-crafts show (616/857-1701). July brings Saugatuck's annual Harbor Day/ Venetian Night with an arts-and-crafts show by day, a lovely lighted boat parade in the evening and fireworks at dusk.

Planning Your Visit to Grand Haven

For more information, contact: Grand Haven/Spring Lake Visitors Bureau (800/303-4096; 616/842-0379 fax; or www.grandhaven chamber.org).

LODGINGS

Brand-name lodgings crop up along US-31. Independent properties include: Harbor House Inn—Overlooking the Grand River, this Victorian bed and breakfast has 17 rooms,

some with fireplaces and whirlpools. Doubles from $120 (800/841-0610). Boyden House Inn—This 1874 Victorian inn near downtown houses original art and eclectic furnishings. Some of the seven rooms have whirlpool baths. Doubles from $85 (616/846-3538). Khardomah Lodge— Green awnings shade this 1873 white frame inn near downtown, just 300 yards from Lake Michigan and Grand Haven State Park. Its 16 simple rooms share five baths. Guests can use the kitchen, dining room and great-room with its fieldstone fireplace. Doubles from $49 a night (616/842-2990).

CAMPING

Grand Haven State Park—On the city's western edge, this park offers beachside camping among its 167 modern sites. P.J. Hoffmaster State Park, 5 miles north, has beaches, dunes and hiking trails near 297 modern sites (616/798-3711 for both; 800/44-PARKS for reservations).

DINING

Bil-Mar Restaurant—This 40-year-old downtown favorite with a deck overlooking Lake Michigan serves steaks, fried perch and walleye (616/842-5920). Kirby Grill—Grab an outdoor table at this bistro in the downtown waterfront district. The building dates to the 1840s, but the menu features contemporary pastas (616/846-3299). Morning Star Cafe— Open daily for breakfast and lunch only, serving southwestern cuisine, plus bread pudding and other homemade desserts (616/844-1131).

SIGHTSEEING

Harbor Steamer paddle wheeler—Cruise the Grand River and Spring Lake; board at downtown Chinook Pier. Rates are $5 to $10 for adults, $2.50 to $5 for 17 and under (616/842-8950). The Harbor Trolley— Depart Chinook Pier for half-hour narrated tours of Grand Haven and Spring Lake, 11 a.m. to 10 p.m. daily during summer. Rates: $2 for 13 years and up, $1 for kids and seniors (616/842-3200). The Gillette Visitor Center—In P.J. Hoffmaster State Park just north of Grand Haven in Muskegon, join in organized nature walks and other activities to learn how the dunes formed (616/798-3573).

ACTIVITIES

Fishing—Michigan requires fishing licenses for anglers 16 and older;

bait shops and charter captains sell one-day licenses. These charters set out from Grand Haven seeking Chinook salmon, steelhead trout and other sport fish. Rates average $280 for a 6-hour trip for four: Bolhouse Charter Service (616/361-0704 or 616/846-1076); Lazy J Charters (616/842-5725 or 800/237-5725); Tammy Too Charters (800/824-2343); Whitney Charters (616/846-1539); Wild Irish Charters (616/847-9300). Boating—Take a captained voyage with Craig Porter Sailboat Charter in Grand Haven. Rates: $95 an hour for party of six (616/846-4032). Or rent jet skis, motor boats, pontoons and fishing boats at Paradise Cove Boat Rentals in Spring Lake. Rates are $45 to $80 an hour (616/842-3713). Bicycling—Almost 100 miles crisscross the area. Bike rentals are $5 to $8 per hour at Buffalo Bob's in downtown Grand Haven (616/847-0019) or Rock 'n' Road Cycle on the north side of town just off US-31 (616/846-2800). Golfing—The 18-hole public courses include: Grand Haven Golf Club, which spans pines and dunes (616/842-4040), and West Shore Golf Club overlooking Lake

Michigan in Douglas (616/857-2500).

FESTIVALS

The Trillium Festival, held at P.J. Hoffmaster State Park each May, pays tribute to the delicate white wildflowers that pop up in profusion along the sand dunes (616/798-3573). Coast Guard Festival— The whole town joins in Grand Haven's July event with Coast Guard cutter tours and buoy tender, nightly concerts, a juried arts-and-crafts fair, a parade and fireworks (800/303-4097).

Visiting Holland

A strong Dutch presence prevails in Holland (population: 30,000) along Lake Macatawa 4 miles from Lake Michigan. Its roots date to the mid-1800s, when Dutch settlers en route to Wisconsin stayed to farm land here instead. Today, an ancient 12-story windmill from Holland dominates Windmill Island, set off each spring by brilliant red and yellow tulips.

Downtown Holland charms with red brick sidewalks fronting low-slung, lace-curtained brick and wood frame buildings. Listed on the National Register of Historic Places, it boasts more than 150 shops, restaurants and services, many of them along Eighth St. and River Ave. On summer evenings, the Art Deco band shell resounds with the American Legion band's marches and pop music.

Holland looks to its heritage each May when countless colorful blooms provide the backdrop for Tulip Time, a 10-day celebration of music, dance and horticulture. The Volksparade puts

Holland, Michigan, charms visitors with Old World architecture and traditional Dutch crafts and cookery.

the townfolk in traditional Dutch costume for an actual street-scrubbing (800/822-2770).

Gardeners can procure bulbs from the 80-acre Veldheer Tulip Farm, 4 miles north of the city along US-31. At factories here, artisans produce delicate blue-and-white delft china, as well as *klompen*, the traditional Dutch wooden shoes (616/399-1900).

At the Original Wooden Shoe Factory on Holland's east side, watch crafters fashion

logs into footwear or browse shops displaying Dutch chocolates, cheeses and other imported delicacies. (616/396-6513).

Stroll beside canals in Dutch Village, a 10-acre theme park that replicates 19th-century Netherlands. Nearby, the reed-roofed Queen's Inn, serves *erwtensoep* (pea soup) and other Dutch treats (616/393-0310).

Holland State Park

claims frontage on both Lake Michigan and Lake Macatawa. Hiking trails thread through the park and its 374 campsites (616/399-9390). The beach on the north side of the channel offers a view of the Big Red lighthouse.

Contact: Holland Area Convention & Visitors Bureau (616/394-0122; 800/506-1299; 800/757-7552 for lodging; or www.holland.org/hcvb).

LODGINGS

Sunset Harbor Cottages—Amenities for

11 units include picnic tables, grills, clubhouse, tennis and volleyball courts, and access to a bike path. The cottages are located near Holland State Park. Doubles from $65 (616/399-9626).

North Shore Inn— This intimate bed and breakfast with three guest rooms offers a wide lawn sloping down to Lake Macatawa, where a paddleboat awaits. Doubles from $100 (616/394-9050).

Centennial Inn— This downtown 1889 Victorian residence served as Holland's first hospital. Stay in the main house or carriage house. Doubles from $100 (616/355-0998).

DINING

Alpen Rose Restaurant & Pastry Shop—Try Viennese pastries or a Bavarian-style dinner with specialties such as Wiener schnitzel and sauerbraten (616/393-2111).

Black River Bistro & Brewing Co.—This downtown eatery serves steaks, pastas and gourmet pizzas (616/394-3000).

The Piper—Whitefish and wood-fired pizzas are served in this estab-lishment overlooking Lake Macatawa (616/335-5866).

By Carol Guensburg

LUDINGTON AND MANISTEE

Nestled between Lake Michigan and vast stretches of forest are the towns that timber built.

Gussied-up Victorian houses preen in pleasing contrast to the glistening waters and inviting woodlands that embrace the port cities of Ludington and Manistee, midway up Michigan's Lower Peninsula. Ludington, with 8,700 residents, hugs Lake Michigan and the northern shore of Pere Marquette Lake, 95 miles north of Grand Rapids. Thirty miles farther north, Manistee (population: 7,000) straddles the Manistee River between the big lake and inland Manistee Lake.

The two communities trace their origins to the mid-1800s, when their lumber mills and ships fed a growing country's demand for housing. Stands of white pine, cedar and ancient hardwoods fell, yielding many of the multistoried, gabled homes that add character to both cities. Manistee treasures its legacy of 19th-century architecture and proudly calls itself the "Victorian Port City." Ludington's refurbished Victorian belles flank the main street that cuts straight west through town and heads, like most visitors, directly to the shore.

Manistee: Romancing the Past

In the 1880s, Manistee's thriving lumber industry made it Lake Michigan's third-largest port after Chicago and Milwaukee. Today, its lakefront beach teems with volleyball games, sand castle construction and scavenging gulls. Cameras click as visitors photograph the Fifth Avenue Beach lighthouse and its graceful iron catwalk, parts of which date to 1855. Only three other catwalks remain on the Lower Peninsula's western shore.

Downtown, a handsome riverwalk diverts attention from the lake to the Manistee River. The riverwalk borders almost 1.5 miles of the southern bank, from US-31 west past downtown shops and restaurants and out to First Street Beach.

Streets in and around downtown abound with the legacy of its lumber baron days—Victorian-era architecture that includes charming "painted ladies." Colorfully painted and carefully restored, these homes earn Manistee its Victorian nickname.

JOHN STRAUSS

Buildings along River Street in Manistee hint at the city's 19th-century prosperity.

Take time to poke around the rambling Manistee County Historical Museum along River Street, Manistee's winding main thoroughfare. Every family in town seems to have donated something to this treasure house of a museum. Alongside charming turn-of-the-century toys and World War I army uniforms, you'll find a complete 1903 drug store.

Foot-sore tourists can climb aboard the Manistee County trolley for an hour-long narrated tour of the city. Among the landmarks dotting the route is the raspberry-red 1888 fire hall, the oldest continuously operating fire station in Michigan. The 1903 Ramsdell Theatre, where James Earl Jones launched his acting career, still stages performances within its gilded arch. Be sure to step into the 1892 First Congregational Church to admire the light filtering through prized Tiffany windows.

Manistee's name means "Spirit of the Woods" in the Chippewa language, and outside of town, the woodland setting provides opportunities for hiking, picnicking and more. Two miles north is Orchard Beach State Park, with a sweeping view of Lake Michigan from a bluff-top apple orchard. The park includes swimming, picnic areas and camping.

One-fourth mile farther north, visit the 76-acre Lake Bluff Audubon Center's wildflower garden and an arboretum sheltering a champion sequoia and other non-native trees. Just east of Manistee Lake lies the 910,000-acre Huron-Manistee National Forest, with 16 campgrounds and more than 400 campsites. The North Country Scenic Trail, which winds through the upper tier of the U. S., slices through these woods, as do routes for mountain biking, cross-country skiing and canoeing.

Ludington: An Angler's Eden

Water brings warm-weather crowds to Ludington. The *S. S. Badger*, a massive car ferry the length of 1½ football fields, deposits up to 620 passengers and 180 vehicles after its 4-hour crossings from Manitowoc, Wisconsin. The ferry operates mid-May through mid-October.

At Ludington's Stearns Park, sunbathers plant bright-hued towels on the beach and splash in the big lake's blue-green swells. Nearby, leafy oak trees and a scattering of picnic tables provide a shady alternative.

Fishing boats crisscross the busy harbor, plying the deep, cold lake with sonar equipment, rods and tackle. Ludington holds the state record for trout and salmon catches from a single

Historic White Pine Village, Ludington.

JOHN STRAUSS

JOHN STRAUSS

Manistee's firehouse is a 19th-century treasure.

port. Not surprisingly, more charter fishing boats originate here, too; the fleet numbers about 40.

Anglers casting for walleye, pike, bass, perch and panfish head to the area's intriguing inland waterways. The wild and scenic Pere Marquette River challenges fishing enthusiasts and lures canoers and kayakers. Another option is 12-mile-long Hamlin Lake, Michigan's largest manufactured lake. Loggers created it by damming the Sable River to float logs to the sawmill. Now Hamlin Lake Dam controls the lake level, maintaining prime spots for fishing, swimming, boating and a smattering of resorts.

For a water adventure that takes a look at the past, paddle your way up the canoe trail. You'll pass an abandoned logging camp and explore shallow bayous that attract herons, ducks and other wildlife.

Hamlin Lake, Big Sable River and Lake Michigan pool their charms in Ludington State Park, just 8 miles north of the city. Each summer, more than 750,000 visitors roam its 5,300 acres of sand dunes and beaches, conifers and hardwoods. It's the state's most popular camping destination, with three campgrounds and 344 sites. Stop

in at the visitor center for information about dune walks and naturalists' talks, or set off on 18 miles of intersecting footpaths. (In winter, the park grooms 16 miles of cross-country ski trails.)

History buffs flock to White Pine Village, a settlement 2 miles south of Ludington that re-creates Mason County life from 1850 to 1940. Drop into Abe Nelson's blacksmith shop—or any of the other meticulously restored structures—and a costumed staffer will fill you in on period details.

Stop at the Town Hall's old-fashioned ice cream parlor, where smiling clerks scoop treats. There are maritime and lumbering museums on the grounds, too, along with a research library rich in manuscripts, photographs and other archives.

Village life takes on new excitement during the Civil War muster in July and on select days from May through October, when the Ludington Mariners Old Time Base Ball Club hits and runs on the village green.

When you're ready to leave horse-and-buggy days behind, consider taking to the skies for an overview of Ludington and the surroundings from a seaplane. The flight is a thrill even the wealthiest lumber baron couldn't have bought.

Planning Your Visit to Ludington

For information, contact: Ludington Area Chamber of Commerce (800/542-4600).

LODGINGS

Chain motels hug US-10 east of Ludington. Other options: Snyder's Shoreline Inn—Most of the 44 rooms of this adult-only inn offer lake views from the balconies or patios. Each room has distinctive decor, from stenciling to handmade quilts. From $69, with a two-night minimum on summer weekends (616/845-1261 or 616/843-4441 fax). Four Seasons Lodging—In the downtown Victorian area, this inn has 33 rooms, including four suites. Amish-built country furnishings decorate the inn. Doubles from $67 (616/843-3448; 800/968-0180). Miller's Lakeside Motel—These 52 simply appointed rooms are close to the car ferry, restaurants and shopping; heated outdoor pool. From $69 (616/843-3458). Schoenberger House—This 1903 neoclassical-style bed and breakfast in Ludington has wood trim in white oak, mahogany, cherry, sycamore and black walnut. Each of the five guest rooms has a private bath. Doubles from $120 (616/843-4435). Sauble Resort on Hamlin Lake—Cottages 5 miles north of Ludington rent by the week. Rates: $385 for two bedrooms, $543 for three bedrooms, $620 for four bedrooms. Heated swimming pool, shuffleboard, tennis courts and game room are available (616/843-8497).

CAMPING

Ludington State Park—344 modern sites with electrical hookups are $15 per night. Call Michigan's state parks central reservation service: 800/44-PARKS. (Vehicles require $4 daily pass or $20 annual state park sticker.)

DINING

PM Steamers—Overlooking the marina and car ferry, this place is known for its nut-encrusted walleye and "fish in a bag," a combination of orange roughy, crab and shrimp cooked in parchment (616/843-9555). House of Flavors Restaurant—A soda fountain and juke box add '50s flair to sandwiches, fries and 41 flavors of ice cream. The adjacent dairy ships ice cream nationwide to the Hard Rock Cafe and others (616/845-5785). Gibbs Country House Restaurant—Since 1947 this 350-seat, family-style restaurant along US-10 3 miles east of downtown has served up Swiss steak, roast chicken, sticky buns, homemade cakes and pies. Look for the 15-foot salad bar (616/845-0311). Scotty's—Lake perch, whitefish and prime rib dinners remain favorites at this casual fine-dining restaurant just east of the city limits along US-10 (616/843-4033). Old Hamlin Restaurant—Downtown since 1926, it has built its reputation on great bread and the Plevalean, a low-fat, cherry-flavored burger served on a bun (616/843-4251).

SIGHTSEEING

The *S.S. Badger* car ferry between Ludington and Manitowoc, Wisconsin, operates mid-May through mid-October. One-way fares for cars, vans and pickups $45, $90 round-trip; bicycles $5, $10 round-trip. Passenger rates, in addition to vehicle fares, adults $37, $59 round-trip; lower rates for seniors and children (800/841-4243). Mason County Aviation—Located along US-10, this service enables up to three passengers to see Ludington from the sky. A 15-minute flight is

$40 (616/843-2049). Scenic Seaplanes—Take a seaplane ride from Sauble Resort along lower Hamlin Lake, just north of Ludington. A 20-minute flight aboard a Cessna 206 starts at $80 for two people (616/845-2877).

ATTRACTIONS

White Pine Village— The 1850–1940 living history settlement southwest of town is open 11 a.m. to 4:30 p.m. Tuesdays-Sundays, Memorial Day to Labor Day. The site closes

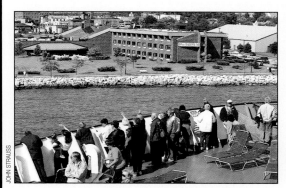

Board the car ferry S. S. Badger to travel between Manitowoc, Wisconsin, and Ludington, Michigan.

30 minutes earlier from mid-April to Memorial Day and from Labor Day to mid-October. $5.50 for adults, $4.50 for youngsters 6 to 17, free for 5 and younger (616/843-4808).

FISHING

In Ludington, 40 captains offer charters. A typical half-day trip starts at $280; $380 for a full day. Call the Ludington

Area Charterboat Association for information about fish, equipment and referrals (616/843-FISH or 800/927-3470). Michigan's Department of Natural Resources issues daily fishing permits and seasonal licenses to residents and nonresidents. Fishing boats and other pleasure craft may dock at the Ludington Municipal Marina (616/843-9611).

SHOPPING

Sunset Bay Antiques— Collectibles, antiques, art and decorative accessories fill 8,000 square feet in the JamesPort Center (616/843-1559). Traverse Bay Woolen Co.—This historic log structure sells warm, colorful blankets from Woolrich, Hudson Bay and Pendleton, as well as furniture and woodland keepsakes (616/843-3540). Artists Market—Across from Ludington's Pere

Marquette Lake, art supplies, pottery, jewelry, prints, photos and hand-decorated mats crowd the market (616/845-6648).

FESTIVALS

The Carferry Festival— This mid-May event kicks off each new season of the S.S. Badger's daily trips to Manitowoc.

South of Ludington

A tiny slice of New England surfaces 15 miles down US-31 from Ludington. Pentwater charms visitors with a traditional village green and clusters of clapboard and brick shops with antiques, art, nautical gifts and fudge. Tackle the 22-mile Hart-Montague Bicycle Trail, then settle in at Gull Landing, a casual dining spot that books live jazz on Sunday evenings and Jimmy Buffet-style performers on select afternoons (616/869-4215).

Enjoy posh lodging and dining at historic Nickerson Inn, up the hill just two blocks west of Charles Mear State Park. Its restaurant offers beef Wellington and quail Chambord on an enclosed porch with a Lake Michigan view. Its bed and breakfast has 10 elegant rooms and two whirlpool suites with fireplaces. From $100 (616/869-8241).

TRAVEL GUIDE

Planning Your Visit to Manistee

For detailed information, contact: Manistee Area Chamber of Commerce (800/288-2286 or www.chamber@ manistee.com).

LODGINGS

Chain motels line US-31 entering Manistee. Others to consider: Milwaukee House— This 1873 inn downtown is Manistee's oldest, offering eight rooms and a two-bedroom suite. From $68 (616/723-7880). 1879 E.E. Douville House—This Victorian "painted lady" near downtown has three guest rooms with period furniture. From $55 (616/723-8654). Lake Shore Motel—On First St. Beach, most of the motel's 20 rooms have great lake views. Doubles from $65; suites from $100; cottages from $300 per week (616/723-2667). Harbor Village—Condo rentals at Fifth Ave. Beach on Lake Michigan are $749 weekly (800/968-0783). Cobi Pines Resort— Three miles south of town, it flanks an 18-hole public golf course and has a pro shop, indoor pool and spa. Doubles from $48, $98 for suites (616/398-0123).

CAMPING

Orchard Beach State Park—Near Manistee, the 174 campsites cost $12 per night. Call Michigan's state parks central reservation service at 800/44-PARKS. (Vehicles require $4 daily pass or $20 annual state park sticker.) Huron-Manistee National Forest—This park has more than 400 campsites. Campers rough it—no electricity or showers. Sites cost from $4 to $10—no reservations needed (616/723-2211; TTY: 616/723-0124).

DINING

Four Forty West—Along the riverwalk by the city marina, dine alfresco on barbecued ribs, lake perch and prime rib (616/723-7902). Gregory's Casual Dining—Along US-31 north of downtown, this family-style restaurant has a lake view and Friday fish specials (616/723-4661). River St. Station—A deck overlooks the Manistee River. The menu includes Reuben sandwiches, prime rib and boutique beers (616/723-8411). Armedo's—Burritos packed with seafood or chicken head the menu at this antique-filled restaurant adjacent to Manistee Lanes bowling alley and

just south of Manistee's city limits along US-31. (616/723-3561). Candy Mountain— Yummy fudge, brittle, caramel corn and dark chocolate-dipped cherries are specialties (616/723-2355).

SIGHTSEEING

Operated by Manistee County Transportation Department, the 55-minute guided trolley tour loops past historic structures and along the river and lakes. $2 for adults, $1 for riders 16

Manistee residents in Victorian costumes gather at an 1870 residence.

and younger or 65 and older (616/723-6525). Orchard Beach Aviation—Take a 12-minute flight in a Cessna 172. $15 for adults, $10 for youngsters. East of the city along US-31 (616/723-8095). Water Bug Tours of the Manistee River—A canvas-topped launch takes 1-hour tours from inland Manistee Lake to the lighthouse and back.

Adults $8; children $4 (616/889-3378).

ATTRACTIONS

Manistee County Historical Museum— Learn about genealogy and Great Lakes maritime history. Admission $1.50 (616/723-5531). Ramsdell Theatre— Manistee Civic Players present year-round concerts and performances on this 1902 stage (616/723-9948 box office). First Congregational Church—Designed by Chicago architect William LeBaron Jenney, tours from 1 to 4 p.m. Wednesdays and Saturdays from mid-June through Labor Day. Donations welcome (616/723-5361). Lake Bluff Audubon Center—This 76-acre site includes the manor home of Morton salt heir Edward Gray. It's along Lakeshore Road 3 miles north of Manistee. Adults $1 (616/723-4042).

FISHING

Manistee County Sport Fishing Association— Events include the Ten Grand Tournament and Budweiser Pro Am, with $50,000 in prizes. The association has information about 30 charter-boat operators who take anglers on fully equipped boats. Half-day excursions average

$300; full-day, 9-hour trips, $450 (616/398-3474). Solberg Marina & Fisherman's Center— The 10 boats based here offer a "no fish, no fee" guarantee on full-day trips (616/723-2611). Manistee Municipal Marina—Pleasure craft may dock here (616/723-1552).

DOWNTOWN SHOPPING

Cornerstone Antiques— In an 1891 building, 20 dealers display dolls, glassware, linens and more (616/398-9089). Hollyhock—Find lamps, throws, picture frames and decorative pillows (616/723-2051). Hitching Post Christmas & Gift Shop—A selection of ornaments includes one replicating the city's lighthouse and catwalk (800/851-5919). Sandpiper—Gourmet foods, souvenirs, nautical-themed gifts and home accessories are found here (616/723-9866).

FESTIVALS

The National Forest Festival on July Fourth weekend features a Venetian boat parade, a powwow, canoe tours, hikes and more. The Victorian Sleighbell Parade is the highlight of Old Christmas Weekend the first of December. Costumed carolers, candlelight house tours, concerts of Handel's "Messiah" and "A

Christmas Carol" dinner contribute to the fun.

North of Manistee

The resort town of Onekama perches on the northeast shore of Portage Lake, about 12 miles north of Manistee and just west of US-31. Follow the Lake Michigan Circle Tour Scenic Drive to clapboard cottages, endless dunes, and prime fishing and swimming waters. A few miles farther north is Bear Lake, home to dozens of resorts, riding stables, and hiking and biking trails.

Head 6 miles southeast to Kaleva to see how the old Finnish community holds time in a bottle: The 1940s Bottle House, constructed from 60,000 pop bottles, is now a museum.

Onekama's Portage Point Inn & Yacht Club, cradled between the dunes and beaches of Lake Michigan and Portage Lake, is a turn-of-the-century white frame resort on the National Historic Register. Dine on bourbon steak, broiled whitefish and other north-woods fare. Doubles from $85 a night, weekly cottage rentals from $670 (616/889-4222; 800/878-7248).

By Carol Guensburg

TRAVERSE CITY, MICHIGAN

Miles of beaches and acres of cherries surround this tourist-friendly town.

Someone long ago dubbed the Lower Peninsula of Michigan "the mitten," an apt description of this land mass shaped by the surrounding Great Lakes. But up in the northwestern corner, Michigan really looks more like a glove, its fingers splayed wide, every crack and crevice filled with Caribbean-hued bays in shimmering bands of turquoise and teal.

At the foot of Grand Traverse Bay—right between the pinkie and the ring finger—Traverse City anchors this sparkling playground of water. One of the Midwest's most prized vacation destinations, its year-round population of 70,000 swells each summer. Still, this waterfront community manages to balance an enormous array of activities with its sense of community. Maple-canopied residential streets sidle up to a vibrant, historic downtown business district.

Tanned beachgoers stroll along Front Street, Traverse City's main east-west avenue where more than 100 sunny cafes, galleries and shops offer everything from nautical home furnishings to down-home cherry pies. Around the corner on Union Street, a cobblestone street marks Old Town, where you'll find more delightful homegrown wares. While window shopping, don't miss the soaring red brick facade of the Opera House at 112 East Front Street. Built in 1882, this Victorian beauty is being restored to its original splendor and hosts a variety of community events.

Head to the Shore

Just a short walk from downtown, sailboat halyards clang rhythmically in the marina, and the calm waters of Grand Traverse Bay shift colors like a lazy chameleon warming in the sun.

On summer days, the bay hums with activity. Tall ships scud by on the breeze, their huge wooden masts creaking from the pull of full sails. Kayaks ply the shoreline. Impromptu fleets of fishing boats hunt for the bay's legendary brown trout; other anglers try their luck at the mouth of the Boardman River, which twists gently through town before melting into Grand Traverse Bay. In spring and fall, it's a

JOHN ROBERT WILLIAMS

Traverse City looks out on its brilliant blue-green bay.

prime spot to catch the runs of salmon and steelhead. Plenty of marinas and rental operations let you check out this boater's paradise for yourself.

Golden beaches arc along the belly of the bay, where toddlers squeal with delight in the soft sand and adults wade in for a refreshing dip. Dozens of hotels and motels along busy US-31 have some of the best beaches right outside their doors. You'll also find easy beach access right downtown at Clinch Park and at West End Beach, where you may want to join a pickup game of sand volleyball.

The Abundant Countryside

The needle-nosed Old Mission Peninsula points north from Traverse City and neatly divides Grand Traverse Bay in two. This whaleback ridge stretches 18 miles, a quiet agrarian landscape striped with cherry orchards and vineyards. No place else on earth grows more cherries per acre than the Old Mission Peninsula.

Veer onto a country road off State-37 and you're likely to spot row after row of reddish-barked trees, some young and spindly, others gnarled and sturdy, drooping under the weight of luminescent fruit. A rollicking festival each July celebrates the juicy harvest with plenty of pies to eat on the spot and jams to stock up on for the winter.

Grapes also thrive in the same climate. Well-staked vines climb up the hillsides and dip into the folds of the land. Area wineries such as Château Grand Traverse welcome you with tastings and tours. Often the views are as award-winning as the region's wines. At Château Chantal, Bob Begin built a castlelike winery on the crest of the peninsula, offering spectacular views of both arms of Grand Traverse Bay. Stop by on Thursday evenings when the winery hosts live jazz and wine tastings on its outdoor terrace.

The Traverse Bay area's well-contoured terrain, pristine inland lakes and perfect summertime climate have also produced nationally acclaimed golf courses. Golfers can choose from stunning Torch Lake vistas at A-Ga-Ming, the piny fairways of the Arnold

Overlook in Sleeping Bear Dunes National Lakeshore.

JOHN STRAUSS

The golf course at Shanty Creek Resort in Bellaire.

JOHN STRAUSS

Palmer Legend course at Shanty Creek, or the humbling The Bear at Grand Traverse Resort with minute greens and deep, deep bunkers designed by Jack Nicklaus. Farther up the bay's eastern shore near Petoskey, the new courses at Bay Harbor already have been deemed among the nation's finest. Designed by Arthur Hills, the 27 holes ramble atop 160-foot bluffs, through natural sand dunes and along the shoreline of Little Traverse Bay for more than 2 miles.

The Lure of the Leelanau

West of Traverse City, the gentle Leelanau Peninsula beckons you to explore its ragged shores and old seafaring towns. In Leland, charter captains string up passengers' catches on the docks at "Fishtown," next to weathered gray fish shanties and nets drying in the sun. The restored 19th-century shanties now house gift shops and eateries, along with venerable Carlson's Fisheries, where you still can buy freshly smoked trout and whitefish right out of the long deli case.

Near the end of the peninsula in Northport, many of the 1860s buildings close to the protected marina have been transformed into eclectic antiques and clothing shops. After browsing, stop by Leelanau State Park, where the peninsula narrows down to a single point and meets the water at the Grand Traverse Lighthouse.

No trip to the Leelanau is complete without exploring Sleeping Bear Dunes National Lakeshore, a 37-mile-long wonder of forests and immense pyramids of sand spiking up along the Lake Michigan shore. Glaciers and a millennium of wind and water sculpted this landscape, now preserved as a 71,000-acre national park. Follow the 7-mile Pierce Stocking Drive to stop at overlooks and follow self-guided walks that teach you about the dune's fragile and unique ecosystems. Kids especially love the Dune Climb, where they can scramble up and down a great barren hill of sand. Hike the trails south of Empire for a view of the tallest dunes—at 450 feet, believed to be the largest outside the Sahara Desert. In the Grand Traverse Bay region, vacation fun comes on a grand scale.

Planning Your Visit to Traverse City

For lodgings reservations and information about the area, contact: Traverse City Convention & Visitors Bureau (800/TRAVERS).

LODGINGS

The Grand Traverse region abounds with beach motels, bed and breakfasts, condominiums and large resorts. Rates listed here are for one-night stays in the summer months. Be sure to ask about packages, especially in the off-season. In Traverse City, US-31 stretching east to Acme is known as "the strip," with a wide-ranging assortment of hotels and motels, many backing up to the sandy beaches of the Grand Traverse Bay's east arm. A few lodging choices to try along the strip and elsewhere:

Grand Beach Resort Hotel—This US-31 lodging has 95 rooms/suites and a private beach on East Grand Traverse Bay. Choose from seven types of rooms, including family suites. Enjoy the indoor pool and game and exercise rooms. Doubles from $148 (800/968-1992).

Waterfront Inn—This waterfront complex in Traverse City offers family activities along a 775-foot beach, indoor pool and kitchenettes. Many of the 128 rooms have bay views. Doubles from $143 (800/551-9283).

Park Place Hotel—A beautifully restored landmark hotel in downtown Traverse City, it boasts great views, an indoor pool and a health club. Doubles from $125 (800/748-0133).

L'Da Ru Lakeside Resort—These lakeside cottages with full kitchens are 10 minutes southwest of Traverse City. Weekly rates from $300 (616/946-8999).

Château Chantal—Part of a winery set high on the Old Mission Peninsula, this unusual inn offers guest rooms with views of the east and west arms of Grand Traverse Bay. Doubles from $105 (800/969-4009).

Open Windows—A white picket fence and English gardens surround a century-old farmhouse with three guest rooms and private baths. It's northwest of Traverse City in Suttons Bay. Doubles from $95 (800/520-3722).

The Homestead—These condominiums along and near Lake Michigan are close to Sleeping Bear Dunes National Lakeshore. The lodge and shoreside inn were added in 1998. Doubles from $83 (616/334-5000).

Grand Traverse Resort—This sprawling full-service resort near Acme has hotel rooms, condominiums, four pools, tennis, golf, health club, children's activity center and more. Doubles from $199 (800/748-0303).

Bayshore Resort—Centrally located and overlooking West Bay, this smoke-free Victorian-style resort offers a game room, guest laundry and corner suites. Doubles from $110 (800/634-4401).

Crystal Mountain Resort—This family-oriented resort stands amid forested hills southwest of Traverse City near Thompsonville. It includes lodge rooms and condominiums, golf, tennis courts, indoor pool, children's activities and more. Doubles from $69 (800/968-7686).

Shanty Creek—This 600-room ski and summer resort northeast of Traverse City near Bellaire features golf, tennis, fitness center, indoor/outdoor pools and more. Doubles from $84 (800/678-4111.)

CAMPING

State Parks—Two state parks offer sites near the water. What Traverse City State Park lacks in privacy it makes up for in convenience, with 344 modern sites near downtown Traverse City along US-31 and a pedestrian overpass to the state park beach area. At the tip of the Leelanau Peninsula, Leelanau State Park has primitive sites along the water near the Grand Traverse Light. Reservations are recommended; these parks fill up fast in summer (800/44-PARKS).

atmosphere overlooking the Bower's Harbor marina (616/223-4030). Bower's Harbor Inn—Ask about the resident ghost at this elegant dining spot on the Old Mission Peninsula. Admire bay views at sunset (616/223-4222). The same building also houses

cuisine, an extensive wine list and exquisite desserts (616/941-0100). Dill's Olde Towne Saloon—A 110-year-old building houses this casual restaurant known for slow-roasted barbecue ribs with cherry barbecue sauce and revue-style entertainment (616/947-7534). Mars Cafe—This small storefront in Traverse City features no-frills, high-quality eats—deli sandwiches, fresh soups, vegetarian selections and coffee bar (616/941-1190). Cousin Jenny's—This downtown Traverse City cafe and tearoom features authentic Cornish pasties, salads, hearty soups and homemade scones (616/941-7821). Old Mission Tavern—Filled with works of local artists, this reasonably priced Old Mission Peninsula spot boasts classic international cooking and daily pasta specialties. See more art in the adjoining Bella Galleria (616/223-7280). The Cove—With expansive decks and windows overlooking "Fishtown" in Leland, it features seafood chowder, fish stew and freshwater fish specialties (616/256-9834). Blue Bird—Moderately priced seafood, homemade soups and a good wine list are found here by the river in Leland (616/256-9081). Next

The majestic tall ship Manitou sails off Sleeping Bear Dunes National Lakeshore, near Empire.

DINING

Apache Trout Grill—This fun and funky Traverse City spot overlooks West Grand Traverse Bay and serves "northern waters" fish specialties partnered with distinctive sauces (616/947-7079). Boathouse—One of the region's most highly touted restaurants, it offers fine and diverse cuisine in a nautical

the more casual and less expensive Bowery, with great ribs, fish and hickory rotisserie chicken (616/223-4333). Sleder's—This Traverse City institution since 1882 features burgers, Mexican dishes and a Friday fish fry (616/947-9213). Windows—This spot overlooking West Grand Traverse Bay boasts distinctive French-American

JOHN STRAUSS

door, the Early Bird is a favorite breakfast spot (616/256-9656).

SIGHTSEEING

Interlochen Center for the Arts—This world-renowned music school and festival site south of Traverse City hosts a music camp and performances by acclaimed musicians in an outdoor pavilion on the shores of Green Lake. Call for a schedule and ticket information (616/276-6230).

Music House—Rare antique mechanical musical instruments at this museum in Acme include music boxes, nickelodeons, jukeboxes, pipe organs and a hand-carved Belgian dance organ (616/938-9300).

Winery Tours and Tastings—Grapes flourish here, and nearly a dozen wineries dot the Leelanau and Mission peninsulas. Many offer free tastings and tours. Contact: Traverse City Convention & Visitors Bureau (800/TRAVERS).

Gwen Frostic Prints—South of Traverse City in Benzonia, visit the eclectic studio and print shop of naturalist, author and artist Gwen Frostic. You can watch the presses at work and purchase her wood-block prints and poetry in this rambling stone-and-wood studio along the banks of the Betsie River

(616/882-5505).

Sleeping Bear Point Coast Guard Station Maritime Museum—In the town of Glen Haven within the national lakeshore, this museum depicts the work of the U.S. Life-Saving Service, the forerunner of today's Coast Guard. Exhibits include life-saving boats and the cannon once used to shoot life lines out to sinking vessels. View video programs illustrating the training and the rigorous life the crews led. The tour is free with national lakeshore admission (616/326-5134).

Tree branches heavy with ripe cherries frame the blue waters of northwest Michigan's Traverse Bay.

Dennos Museum Center—This facility on the campus of North-western Michigan College in Traverse City houses one of the nation's finest collec-tions of Inuit (native peoples of the Canadian Arctic) art, plus interactive exhibits

combining art, science and technology (616/922-1055).

OUTDOOR ADVENTURES

Tall Ship Sailing—An authentic replica of a 19th-century wooden sailing vessel, the tall ship *Malabar* sails the waters of West Grand Traverse Bay three times daily. Sunset sails include a picnic dinner. Also, overnight bed and breakfast packages (800/678-0383).

Golf—Award-winning golf courses include: The Bear at Grand Traverse Resort in Acme (800/748-0303); The Legend at Shanty Creek in Bellaire (800/678-4111); A-Ga-Ming in Kewadin (800/678-0122); and Mistwood in Lake Ann (616/275-5500).

Beaches—From remote spots such as Christmas Cove beach on the Leelanau Peninsula to Clinch Park right in downtown Traverse City, look for great swimming beaches in the region. Empire Beach in the village of Empire offers exceptional views of the Sleeping Bear Dunes to the north. Contact: Traverse City Convention & Visitors Bureau (800/TRAVERS).

Canoeing—Great rivers for paddling wind through the region. Try the Crystal River from Fisher Lake, with rentals from Crystal River Canoe Livery (616/334-3090) or the Platte River, with rentals from the Riverside Canoe Livery between Empire and Frankfort (616/325-5622).

Loda Lake Wildflower Sanctuary—Located within the Manistee-Huron National Forest, this sanctuary protects native Michigan plants, including several endangered and threatened species. The setting comprises a small lake, a marsh and high, dry ground. Walk the easy 1-mile loop on a self-guided tour that points out trillium, pink lady's slipper, swamp rose, water lily, native orchid, Michigan holly and many other species. Obtain a trail guide from a ranger station (616/745-4631; 800/281-8730).

FESTIVALS

The granddaddy of all Traverse Bay festivals is the National Cherry Festival, which celebrates the cherry harvest each July with parades, band competitions, cherry contests, fireworks, Native American pow-wows and plenty of tasting opportunities (616/947-4230). The Boats on the Boardwalk event lines up classic wooden boats on the Boardman River in Traverse City the first weekend of August (800/TRAVERS). The Leland Wine and Food Festival hosts wine tastings, food booths and music at Leland Harbor in June (616/256-9382). The Tall Ship Rally in June brings together local tall ships *Malabar*, *Manitou*, *Madeline* and others, along with a rib cook-off to whet appetites in Traverse City's Open Space (616/946-2723). The August Suttons Bay Art Fair is known as one of the finest shows in northern Michigan, exhibiting the works of the area's celebrated artists (616/271-3050).

WINTER ACTIVITIES

The Grand Traverse region's hilly terrain and abundant lake-effect snow make it one of the premier downhill ski destinations in the Midwest. Downhill resorts include Sugar Loaf Resort in Cedar (800/952-6390); Shanty Creek in Bellaire (800/678-4111); Crystal Mountain in Thompsonville (800/968-7686); and, a little farther north, the sister resorts of Boyne Mountain and Boyne Highlands (800/GO-BOYNE).

Many of the same resorts also provide top-notch cross-country facilities. Shanty Creek's excellent trail network sprawls across a staggering 5,000 acres of woodlands. You even can ski between Shanty Creek's two downhill areas, 13 kilometers apart; a complimentary shuttle will return you to your starting point. Crystal Mountain's Nordic system ranks as one of the finest in the Midwest, with 30 kilometers of impeccably groomed cross-country terrain, including the Screaming Eagle, a 4-kilometer eye-opener that qualifies as a double-black diamond descent. On the Leelanau Peninsula, The Homestead features trails that hug the Lake Michigan shore and link up with nearly 50 kilometers of trails in the wild and windswept Sleeping Bear Dunes National Lakeshore. There are plenty of public trails around Traverse City.

By Tina Lassen

LAKE HURON

Hospitable Lake Huron is the vital link in the Great Lakes chain. At its northwestern end, this second largest of the lakes receives the waters of Lake Superior through the St. Mary's River, then extends a hand to Lake Michigan through the Straits of Mackinac. Wrapping around the eastern shore of Michigan's Lower Peninsula, Lake Huron curves south to greet Lake Erie through a system of waterways that includes the St. Clair River, Lake St. Clair and the Detroit River.

Where the waters of Lake Huron and Lake Michigan meet, you'll find 5 square miles of never-never land called Mackinac Island. Seventeenth-century French voyageurs paddled its waters, Revolutionary War-era British manned a fort here, and Victorian vacationers built fanciful cottages and whiled away summer afternoons coaxing croquet balls across perfectly-tended lawns. Somehow echoes of all those days remain, giving the island a singular charm.

Head south from Mackinac Island and you're on Michigan's sunrise shore. Down-home vacation pleasures are the draw here and relaxation the rule. Family-run resorts with clean-as-a-whistle cottages and small town restaurants featuring fresh-caught fish and fresh-baked pies bring back memories of carefree summers past.

You'll find a string of Michigan's most memorable lighthouses along the Lake Huron shore. The oldest is the Fort Gratiot Light. Michigan was still a territory when the 80-foot tower at the mouth of the St. Clair River first flashed its comforting beacon in 1829.

Adventurous vacationers may want to take a close-up

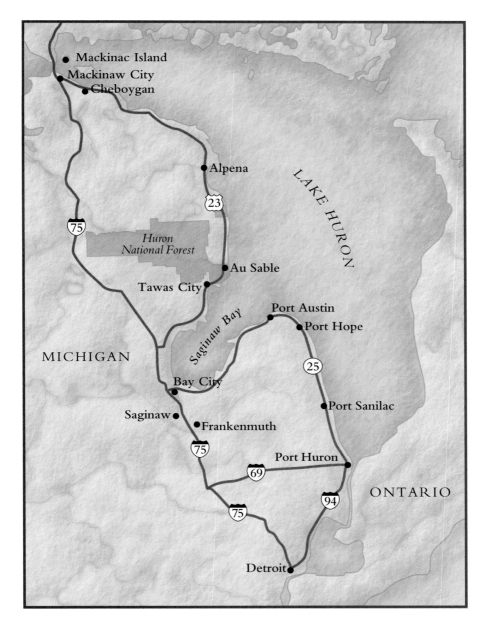

look at the shipwrecks that testify to Lake Huron's darker
side. The Travel Guide on page 121 tells beginning and
experienced divers where to find underwater preserves that
hold the remains of centuries-old ships.

Anglers and antiquers, boaters and beachcombers—
summer's pleasures await them all in Lake Huron's hometown communities and along its unspoiled shoreline.

MACKINAC ISLAND

Gracious hotels and horse-drawn carriages evoke long-ago vacation pleasures.

T he persnickety residents of Michigan's tiny Mackinac Island, who in 1896 banned the smelly, noisy, newfangled automobile from their white-cottaged retreat, did a favor for generations to come. Adrift in the vast sea that is Lake Huron, the pristine green island seems happily suspended in time.

On Your Way to the Past

Mackinac Island (pronounced MACK-i-naw) rises like an emerald from the teal-blue waters of the Straits of Mackinac at the top of Michigan, 300 miles north of Detroit. The straits link Lake Huron and Lake Michigan and separate lower Michigan from its Upper Peninsula, both visible in the misty distance.

The 3½-mile-long bluff-topped island of 470 year-around residents teems with tourists from early May to November. Getting there is half the adventure. The step back in time begins at the I-75 towns of Mackinaw City and St. Ignace on either side of the 5-mile-long Mackinac Bridge. Leave your car—and your cares—on the mainland and board a jet-boat ferry to the village at the island's southern tip.

Visitors crowd the boat's outside decks, leaning into the lake breeze, eager for a first look at the storybook island ahead. The trip takes just minutes, but the island has the feeling of a world apart.

The surrounding Straits of Mackinac were a watery highway for Michigan's earliest settlers. Great Lakes Indians camped along the shoreline and fished the straits' cold depths. Daring voyageurs paddled its waters. French and British traders established outposts and fought to retain the rich, wild lands.

By the late 1800s, word of the island's cool breezes and crystal-clear waters brought vacationers from the Midwest's growing cities. They built gingerbread-trimmed cottages and summer homes, many of which still stand amid manicured gardens along the bluffs. Fearing that motorized carriages would spoil their peace and quiet, residents passed the island's law: No motorcars allowed.

The rule stands, and the hectic and noisy 20th century intrudes very little on Lake Michigan's grande dame of summer resort islands.

MICHAEL SLAUGHTER

A musical afternoon on the broad front lawn of the Grand Hotel.

Mackinac's Many Delights

On a bright mid-summer morning, a gray mare named June and her harness-mate, Smokey, ease a wagon full of visitors along Main Street of Mackinac Island's harbor village. Sharing the busy streets with creaking fringe-topped carriages are bicycles and pedestrians searching for the next souvenir shop.

Along Main and Huron streets, dozens of shops sell everything from snuggly woolens and antique china to rubber tomahawks. Families with kids in strollers linger at fudge-shop windows to watch white-aproned cooks beat and fold 30-pound batches of the irresistible confection that has become synonymous with Mackinac Island.

Away from the shops, vacationers stroll the island's tranquil side streets. Here, gleaming white clapboard hotels, and cottages with whimsical turrets, sweeping verandas and graceful curlicues resemble Victorian ladies done up for a lawn party. Most of these buildings date from the turn of the century when Mackinac Island first became a warm-weather mecca for Midwesterners.

Three Centuries of History

A cannon booms and echoes every half-hour from the walls of Fort Mackinac, looming above the east edge of town. "Soldiers" reenact 18th-century life at this restored outpost that the British Army built to defend the straits against

Bicyclists pedal west of town on Shoreline Road.

DENNIS COX

Victorian homes line the town's pretty side streets.

DENNIS COX

colonists during the Revolutionary War. There are musket firings, fife-and-drum demonstrations and reenactments of courts-martial that took place when American troops occupied the fort.

Costumed interpreters lead children in games dating back a century. In the Discovery Room, youngsters try on soldiers' helmets and pretend they're cooking on an old cast-iron stove. The fort's newest room displays the history of the island from the days of Native Americans to the tourism era.

At the fort's Tea Room, you can order lunch at outdoor tables while you watch ferries dock downtown and tourists and horses amble far below.

The Island's Grand Old Lady

Along Mackinac Island's East Bluff, rippling yellow awnings, fluttering American flags, lush lawns and sculptured flower gardens outline the white frame, century-old Grand Hotel. Although there are more than a dozen other hotels and bed-and-breakfast inns on Mackinac, islanders call the Grand simply "the hotel." It's regally sited, enthroned on 500 acres covered with thousands of blooms (more than 100,000 bedding plants and almost 30,000 tulips and daffodils alone).

"We take you back to a time when the pace was less hurried," explains Mimi Musser, the 325-room hotel's vice president and daughter of the owner.

Built more than a century ago by railroad and steamship barons wanting to attract wealthy vacationers, the inn ranks among the world's largest summer hotels. Designer Carleton Varney has updated the interior with bold summer colors that complement the many antiques.

Meals here are events, five-course feasts served by waiters in formal attire. Guests dress for dinner, too; jackets for men and dresses or pant suits for women are required. Breakfasts showcase more than 30 choices, from fluffy omelets to pastries from scratch, and the lunch buffet stretches almost 100 feet. The parlor is the setting for afternoon tea, and those still on their feet after partaking of the day's meals may dance in the ballroom to the big band sound of the hotel orchestra.

The Grand Hotel's massive front porch, fanned by a steady lake breeze and commanding a noble view of the straits, remains among the world's longest (680 feet). Down its length of two-story stately pillars, hundreds of potted red geraniums flank an army of white wicker rocking chairs, the ideal symbol of the island's relaxed elegance.

Planning Your Visit to Mackinac Island

For more information, contact: Mackinac Island Chamber of Commerce (800-4-LILACS) or TRAVEL MICHIGAN (888/78-GREAT).

GETTING THERE

Ferries to Mackinac Island from Mackinaw City or St. Ignace: Arnold Transit Co. (800/542-8528); Shepler's (800/828-6157); Star Line (800/638-9892). Nearest airport: Pellston, 17 miles south of the ferry docks in Mackinaw City.

LODGINGS

Grand Hotel—(see page 111). Doubles, including breakfast and dinner, from $320 (800/33-GRAND). Island House—Guests view Mackinac Harbor from the broad front porch of this 1852 inn, the island's oldest. Recently refurbished, it offers an indoor heated pool and spa. Doubles from $140 (906/847-3347). Metivier Inn Bed & Breakfast—Sherry is served in the late afternoon at this gracious 1887 Victorian inn with inviting porches. Doubles from $110 (906/847-6234). Mission Point Resort—

At this luxury resort set on 18 acres, guests gather in the grand main lodge where three fireplaces take the nip out of chilly evenings. Doubles from $169 (800/833-7711).

DINING

Woods—In a secluded forest setting away from town, Bavarian decor sets the mood for relaxed dining (906/847-3699). Carriage House Restaurant—There's veranda seating and a view of the straits from this fine dining restaurant in the Iroquois Hotel (906/847-3321). Governor's Dining Room—In the venerable The Island House hotel, this institution long has been considered one of the island's best. Steaks, seafood and chops rate high (906/847-3347). Horn's Gaslight Bar & Restaurant—Locals have been enjoying burgers, soup and other dishes since 1933. There's an ornate old-fashioned wooden bar and a special menu for kids (906/847-6154).

ATTRACTIONS

Ask at your hotel for information about renting bicycles, saddle horses and carriages. Mackinac Island Carriage Tours—The clip-clop of horses enhances a narrated

tour of the island (906/847-3573). Fort Mackinac—See 14 original buildings dating to the Revolutionary War. Excellent costumed interpreters explain it all (906/847-3328). Butterfly House—For a unique encounter with nature, take a short walk from the busy shop scene to Mission Street. Step into a warm, misty greenhouse to find yourself surrounded by hundreds of marvelous butterflies, large and small, exotic and domestic (906/847-3972). Father Marquette National Memorial—History buffs can travel to nearby St. Ignace to visit a museum displaying writings of the priest-explorer Father Marquette and dioramas depicting his life among the Indians of the Heartland (906/847-3328).

SHOPPING

Indulge in fudge. At most shops, you can sample before you buy. Sutler's Store—This Fort Mackinac shop offers interesting items relating to the island's history. See the fine selection of books and pottery by local artists (906/847-3331).

FESTIVALS

Mackinac Island Lilac Festival—The second

week in June, hundreds of fragrant lilacs bloom in abandon, and the island celebrates springtime with events that include a parade (800-4-LILACS).

NATIVE AMERICAN INFLUENCES

Early Great Lakes Indians—the Chippewas, Hurons and others—chose Mackinac as holy ground. They believed the 75-foot limestone pinnacle of Sugar Loaf, at the island's center, and Arch Rock, a massive natural bridge capping a lakeside cliff, were works of the Great Spirit. The intriguing formations still fascinate visitors

Seventeenth-century explorer and Jesuit missionary Père Marquette gazes out at Marquette Park.

who venture beyond Main Street to roam the extensive inland trails.

"The best way to see Mackinac," says Phil Porter, Mackinac Island State Park curator and author of a book about the island's natural setting, "is to get on a bicycle and discover it yourself."

WINTER ACTIVITIES

Traditionally, the island's attractions and hotels are closed during the winter months, with a few exceptions for special holiday events between Christmas and New Year's. In recent years, however, cross-country skiers have discovered the joy of schussing nearly deserted forest trails in the state parks that cover more than 80 percent of the island. A number of lodgings and restaurants stay open to accommodate them.

Places to stay include Pontiac Lodge (906/847-3364) and Harbor Place Apartments (800/626-6304). Among restaurants open during the winter are the Mustang Lounge (906/847-9916) and the Village Inn (906/847-3542).

Great Lakes Air, Inc., makes daily flights to the island from the town of St. Ignace on Michigan's UP (906/643-7165). Horse-drawn taxis (carriages or sleighs, if needed) pick up winter visitors at the airport. Reservations for taxis are recommended (906/847-3323).

For information about winter-season activities, contact: Mackinac Island Chamber of Commerce (800/4-LILACS).

OTHER PLACES TO VISIT IN THE AREA

Mackinaw City

On the mainland, in the shadow of the 5-mile-long Mackinac Bridge, Mackinaw City (population: 875) caters to visitors with shops and casual eateries. Motels and campgrounds accommodate overnight guests (800/666-0160). On Labor Day, the bridge opens to pedestrians for the annual Labor Day Bridge Walk. As many as 60,000 trek its length, from St. Ignace to Mackinaw City (800/338-6660).

Just west of the bridge, redcoats drill once again within the timber walls of reconstructed Colonial Michilimackinac (616/436-5563). In 1715, the French

113

claimed this strategic location overlooking the straits as a military outpost. For the next 50 years, the fort was a hub of the Great Lakes fur trade. Today, it's a state park with more than a dozen painstakingly rebuilt structures.

Heading down the Sunrise Shore on US-23, note white-pine forests and sunlight spilling across the lake. Dawn bathes beaches in shades of amber, as gentle waves tug at the sand. Offshore, charter fishing boats slice through whitecaps. In their wake, gulls greet the morning, swooping on updrafts and diving for the day's freshest catch.

Along the way is evidence of the timber boom that built the towns: Victorian homes built by lumber barons, logging trucks on the byways and mills.

Four miles southeast of Mackinaw City, tour the state's first sawmill and, indeed, its first industrial development, at Mill Creek State Park. Here, Robert Campbell operated his 18th-century mill to satisfy the building boom at Fort Mackinac and Mackinac Island. The staff runs the water-powered mill and demonstrates antique tools (616/436-5564).

Cheboygan

Cheboygan (population: 5,000) straddles Michigan's Inland Waterway. Once Native Americans paddled this chain of lakes, which, with an 8-mile portage, connects Lake Huron with Lake Michigan. Now pleasure boaters cruise the Cheboygan River through the town and up the waterway. Dock beside restaurants such as the 1847 Hack-Ma-Tack Inn (616/625-2919). Be sure to scan the skies for bald eagles soaring overhead. Contact: Cheboygan Chamber of Commerce (800/968-3302).

Rogers City

South on US-23 along Lake Huron's western shoreline is Rogers City

Mackinac Island's century-old no-automobiles rule means visitors travel by horse-drawn "taxis."

(population: 3,600). This community is decidedly nautical, with a wide harbor and sailboats scudding among the waves.

Beneath a green-and-white striped awning along tidy Main Street, Emil Plath welcomes customers to Plath's Meats, famous for its smoked pork loins for more than 85 years (517/734-2232). Sample them at the nearby Buoy Restaurant and Lounge overlooking Lake Huron (517/734-4747). P.H. Hoeft State Park offers camping, a picnic area and Lake Huron beach (517/734-2543).

Presque Isle Lighthouses

Most harbors consider themselves lucky to have one vintage lighthouse, but Presque Isle Harbor between Rogers City and Alpena boasts two: the 1840 Old Presque Isle Lighthouse and the "new" 1860 Presque Isle Lighthouse. When the height and location of the original light-house (now a museum) proved insufficient, another was built 1 mile north. The automated light of the Presque Isle Lighthouse, the tallest along the Great Lakes at 113 feet, still guides mariners (800/4-ALPENA).

Alpena

In the lakeside city of Alpena (population: 11,350), specialty and antiques shops line N. 2nd St. in the Old Town historic district. Visit the Jesse Besser Museum for a view of an 1890s avenue of shops, plus 13th-century copper plates and utensils (517/356-2202).

As in many shore towns, Alpena's timber boom faded in the late 1800s. Elaborate homes built by prominent businessmen pay tribute to the community's second life as a concrete-manufacturing center. Alpena's wide natural harbor has claimed more than its share of shipwrecks. Now designated as the Thunder Bay Underwater Preserve, the harbor shelters more than 80 shipwrecks. The area captivates scuba divers (800/4-ALPENA).

For dinner, locals like the John A. Lau Saloon, a pub serving signature sauce-smothered beef ribs (517/354-6898).

To overnight in the area, consider the Churchill Pointe Inn.

Seven miles off US-23 along Hubbard Lake south of Alpena, this 1927 lakeside inn has fine dining and a long deck overlooking the water (800/727-2078).

South on US-23, just before Harrisville, is the Sturgeon Point Lighthouse. Now being phased out as a beacon, it has guided vessels offshore since 1870. The tower's gleaming white structure with red shutters is open as a museum (517/724-5107).

AuSable and Oscoda

The neighboring communities of AuSable and Oscoda reside on opposite banks of the AuSable River, which winds from north central Michigan near Grayling to empty into Lake Huron. In July, canoeists head here for the annual AuSable Canoe Marathon, a 14-hour race to Oscoda, featuring top U.S. and international athletes (800/235-4625).

A 68-mile driving tour loops through Huron National Forest (517/362-8961). Along the route is the home of the Kirtland warbler, an endangered species. (There are periodic tours for viewing.) The River Road Scenic Byway (800/235-4625) includes the bronze

Lumbermen's Monument and gurgling Largo Springs, a tranquil retreat hidden beneath a canopy of pines, hemlocks and moss-laden bluffs.

A good stop for lunch or dinner here is The Pack House. Set in a comfortable 1878 home, this restaurant is known for specialties such as seafood baked in parchment (517/739-0454). For lakeside lodging, consider Huron House Bed and Breakfast between East Tawas and Oscoda. Guests can relax in a hot tub under the stars. Doubles from $75 (517/739-9255).

East Tawas and Tawas City

East Tawas (population: 2,935) and Tawas City (population: 2,036) cling like twins to the wide, blue expanse of Tawas Bay. On a curve of tree-lined beach, Tawas Point Lighthouse towers above Tawas Point State Park, a 183-acre preserve that campers favor. Beach lovers claim the rolling sands and blanketlike dune grass just beyond the long boardwalk. For information, contact: Tawas Bay Tourist & Convention Bureau (800/55-TAWAS).

By Dixie Franklin

BAY CITY TO PORT HURON

**Around Michigan's "Thumb,"
the towns along Saginaw Bay and
Lake Huron invite you to relax.**

DENNIS COX

T he waters of Saginaw Bay scoop deeply into
Michigan's east coast, sculpting the Thumb of
the mitten-shaped silhouette that defines the state's
Lower Peninsula. The bay flows seamlessly into Lake
Huron, wrapping this sleepy region in idyllic isolation.

Away from the mainstream of summer traffic, the
Thumb's quiet fishing villages, lonely lighthouses and
solitary beaches look much as they have for decades.
Hours are marked by the return of fishing boats,
heavy with the day's catch, and by lengthening
shadows on sugar-sand beaches.

To discover the area's lakeside pleasures, follow the
green-and-white signs of the Lake Huron Circle Tour
Route (State-25). Sweeping views and small towns
characterize the 145-mile route from Bay City to Port
Huron, the bustling, hardworking ports that anchor
each end of State-25.

Beginning in Bay City

Bay City (population: 38,000), at the southwestern
tip of Saginaw Bay, bears little resemblance to the
rip-roaring mill town it was at the end of the 19th
century. The last of the sawmills along the Saginaw
River were razed in the 1930s. Today, freighters from
Russia and the Far East navigate a channel once
choked with logs, making Bay City the state's second
busiest port. Visitors find perfect spots for picnicking
and ship watching along the city's Riverwalk, a 2.5-
mile hiking and biking trail that parallels the Saginaw
River's west bank.

Architecture buffs can wander past more than 250
vintage homes along flower-filled Center Avenue,
opulent mansions that recall the city's lumbering
heyday. A few, including the 1884 Clements Inn, now
serve as welcoming bed and breakfasts. The past also is
on view at Bay City Antiques Center, which takes up
the better part of a city block along Water Street.

The 125-foot clock tower of the 1894 Romanesque-
style city hall dominates the skyline. Inside, a 31-foot
tapestry woven with more than 500 colors depicts the
town's historic buildings. Work your way up the 68 steps
of the clock tower for impressive views of the area.

North of Bay City, the largely undeveloped Albert

Old Port Sanilac
Lighthouse
presides over that
town's harbor.

E. Sleeper State Park boasts 1,000 acres of sunny beach where kids can leap off 30-foot dunes or dip in the surf. Easy-to-follow markers help hikers identify native trees, shrubs and wildflowers along the Ridges Nature Trail.

At nearby 655-acre Port Crescent State Park, families splash in gentle waves along 3 miles of beach. Picnic decks punctuate the boardwalk that weaves among the dunes. Dinner-is-ready aromas drift from campsite grills.

Thumb's Up— the Northern Tip

Sandy beaches and marshlands dominate the sheltered shoreline from Bay City to Port Austin. Inland, tidy bean and sugar beet farms thrive. In Port Austin (population: 1,500) at the Thumb's northern tip, vacationers stroll from bed and breakfasts and neat motels to the half-mile breakwater on Lake Street. It's the perfect spot to catch the sun's twice-daily shows. Purple sunrises explode across Lake Huron; blazing orange sunsets splash across Saginaw Bay, which some label the best in the state.

Take time to tour the now-closed Grindstone City quarries (local residents use the huge old grindstones as lawn art). South of Bad Axe, look for the Sanilac Petroglyphs, dramatic images carved into stone by a prehistoric people.

Lake Huron's savage beauty is apparent on the unsheltered side of Port Austin as you head south on State-25. Jade-colored breakers batter wave-worn cliffs, and rocky shores give way to bluffs offering awe-inspiring views.

Near Port Hope, the Point Aux Barques Light stands watch. A 120-acre park surrounds the graceful white tower, built in 1857 to warn ships away from dangerous shoals. Visitors can tour the keeper's home, now a museum. Port Hope also is the jumping off point for the Thumb Area Bottomland Preserve, a protected shipwreck site open to scuba divers.

At Huron City, a 19th-century lumber town, visit 10 buildings set amid colorful flower beds, including the House of Seven Gables, once the home of the town's wealthy founder.

Heading to Port Huron

In Port Sanilac, a historic lighthouse presides over a modern marina where boats appear to outnumber the year-

Charter fishing on Saginaw Bay.

DENNIS COX

The Loop-Harrison House in Port Sanilac.

DENNIS COX

round population of 700. The village claims 40 buildings more than a century old. At the Sanilac County Historical Museum and Village, costumed guides lead tours of the elaborate Loop-Harrison mansion. Dr. Loop's medicines fill shelves in the vintage doctor's office.

Plan a stop in Lexington, 12 miles south, where luscious berries beckon from roadside stands and farms. Allow time for Mary's Pie Shop, a modest brown cottage with a hand-painted sign and the aroma of fresh-baked pies in the air.

Port Huron (population: 33,700), at Lake Huron's southern tip, is one of Michigan's oldest towns. Its impressive Blue Water Bridge links the city to Sarnia, Ontario. During a normal shipping season, more seagoing tonnage passes under the towering arch than through any channel except the Panama and Suez canals.

The former lumber port is best known, however, as Thomas Edison's hometown. The inventor is honored at the city's Museum of Arts and History, which houses items from Edison's boyhood home. At Thomas Edison Park, under the Blue Water Bridge, is the city's restored train depot, where young Edison boarded the Detroit-bound train to sell fruit, nuts and newspapers. The inventor used his earnings to buy supplies for the small laboratory he had set up in the train's baggage car.

In July, join the crowds heading into town along State-25 for the annual festivities surrounding the three-day Port Huron-to-Mackinac Island yacht race. Along the way, listen for the cries of circling gulls, the jingle of rigging in marinas and the purr of fishing charters heading out. That's the summer song of "Michigan's Secret Shore."

Planning Your Visit to Michigan's "Thumb"

For area information, contact: TRAVEL MICHIGAN (888/78-GREAT); Huron County Visitors Bureau (800/35-THUMB); Bay Area Convention & Visitors Bureau (888/BAY-TOWN); Blue Water Area Convention & Visitors Bureau (800/852-4242). Lodgings are plentiful in the Thumb's larger cities of Bay City and Port Huron. Along the shore in between, places to stay are scarcer, and reservations are recommended on peak summer weekends.

Bay City
LODGINGS

Bay Valley Resort—This is a full-service resort with tennis courts, 150 rooms and a respected par-5, 602-yard double dogleg golf course. There's also a well-run children's program. Doubles from $75 (517/686-3500).

Clements Inn—This lavish Center St. mansion dating to 1886 has been converted into a bed and breakfast. The homemade candlelight breakfasts are extra-special treats, as are the in-room whirlpool suites with fireplaces. Doubles from $70 (800/442-4605).

DINING

For an Upper Peninsula-style meal, check out Yooperville Pasties, which features these Cornish-style specialties baked fresh daily, Trennary cinnamon toast and UP smoked fish (517/684-3899).

Heatherfield's—In the Bay Valley Resort, this restaurant is known for its Sunday brunch and tables overlooking the golf course (517/686-6150).

Krzysiaks House—This well-run family-style restaurant features a hearty lunch buffet, Polish specialties and chicken noodle soup (517/894-5531).

Terry & Jerry's O Sole Mio—This eatery has been serving spaghetti to locals since 1951 (517/893-3496).

SIGHTSEEING

The Historical Museum of Bay County—Trace the development of the area from pre-Columbian times through the 20th century. Housed in a former meeting hall where the Bull Moose Party was founded during Teddy Roosevelt's time, the museum includes exhibit areas such as lavish period rooms and displays about fur trading, lumbering and shipbuilding industries (517/893-5733).

The Bay City State Recreation Area—A 2,800-acre area connects the Frank N. Anderson Nature Trail, the Bay City State Park and the Tobico Marsh State Game Area, a sprawling refuge for more than 100 species of birds and waterfowl (517/667-0717).

Port Austin
LODGINGS

The Garfield Inn—Named after President Garfield, a former guest in this lakeside mansion, it's now a posh bed and breakfast with six rooms and an elegant eatery. Specialties include Bay Port perch, grilled prime rib, home-baked breads and desserts. Doubles from $70 (517/738-5254).

The Castaways—The area's largest family resort has 36 units and 10 comfortable cottages overlooking Saginaw Bay. Amenities include a heated pool, game room, on-site restaurant and 400 feet of sandy beach. Doubles from $82 (517/738-5101). Camping is available at the Port Austin KOA and Resort, on 55 acres 1 mile from the beach. The facilities include a game room, baseball field and volleyball court (517/738-2267).

DINING

The Bank—Enjoy gourmet entrées such as walleye with crabmeat

dressing baked in parchment paper. Finish with homemade desserts, all served in a century-old bank building (517/738-5353).
The Farm Restaurant— Inventive Heartland-style cuisine uses lots of fresh, local ingredients (517/874-5700).
Joe's Pizzeria Italian/American Restaurant—This is the place to head for pasta and pizza (517/738-8711).

dunes (517/738-8663).
Huron City Museum— Check out 10 buildings from the 1850–1890 Victorian era: the LaGasse Log Cabin, Phelps Memorial Church, Point Aux Barques U.S. Lifesaving Station, Hubbard's General Store, Community House/Inn, Brick Museum, a carriage shed, two barns and the House of Seven Gables (the former residence of Langdon Hubbard and

Underwater Preserve, with 163 square miles and wrecks that range from an 1876 steamer to a 1920s tugboat; the Thumb Area Underwater Preserve, with 276 square miles and 10 major ship-wrecks, including the Philadelphia and the Albany, two ships that collided in an 1893 accident; and the 288-square-mile Thunder Bay Underwater Preserve, which has one of the highest densities of shipwrecks per mile of any point on the Great Lakes. Great visibility makes underwater photo-graphy especially popular here. The Nordmeer, a German steamer, sank in 1966 in shallow water, and provides a good start for those with little or no diving experience. Diving companies throughout the Thumb offer charters and lessons for both beginners and advanced divers.

DENNIS COX

The Garfield Inn Bed & Breakfast is named for the U.S. president who once stayed at this Port Austin mansion.

RECREATION & SIGHTSEEING
The Albert E. Sleeper State Park—The park beguiles visitors with 1,003 acres, including a sandy beach. Fishing, hiking and picnicking draw warm-weather visitors; cross-country skiing, winter athletes (517/856-4411).
Port Crescent State Park—More than 500 acres encompass beautiful beaches and miles of nature trails and

later Dr. William Lyon Phelps). Tours are conducted July–Labor Day, closed Tuesdays and Wednesdays (517/428-4123).
Canoeing—Tip-A-Thumb Canoes offers day trips to Port Crescent State Park (517/738-7656).
Shipwrecks—Countless ships have gone down in Lake Huron, many in the area off the Thumb. Divers will be eager to explore three areas: Sanilac Shores

Port Hope
The lighthouse at Point Aux Barques (the name is French for "Point of Boats") has been a landmark since the early days of Great Lakes travel. It presides over the tip of the Thumb where Lake Huron makes a westerly swing into Saginaw Bay. The 89-foot brick tower is closed to the public, but visitors may tour the attached keeper's house, which

includes a museum telling about ships that sank at this treacherous point. The shipwrecks have become popular dive sites, now part of an underwater preserve (800/35-THUMB).

Port Sanilac
LODGINGS
The Raymond House Inn—Seven guest rooms are just 500 feet from Lake Huron. The gracious Victorian bed and breakfast was built in 1871 and has an on-site fitness center. Doubles from $65 (800/622-7229).
The Bellaire Motel— Many say the restaurant here holds the Thumb's best fish fry. The Douros family, owners since 1945, has built a reputation for perch and pickerel dinners, as well as the tart lemon meringue pie (810/622-9981).

Port Huron
LODGINGS
Thomas Edison Inn—This posh inn has 149 rooms and 12 suites, many with stunning views of the bridge and Lake Huron. Doubles from $89 (810/984-8000).
The Victorian Inn— It's an elegant bed and breakfast and a renowned restaurant featuring a menu that changes monthly. Specialties include rack of lamb. A cozy

basement pub is nice for an after-dinner drink. Four rooms upstairs accommodate overnight guests. Doubles from $65 (810/984-1437).

DINING
Fogcutter Restaurant— This is a romantic setting with views of the water and a menu featuring fresh fish and classic fare. The almond shrimp is a house special-ty (810/987-3300).
River Crab Restaurant— Worth the drive south to St. Clair, the River Crab is part of the respected Chuck Muer chain of seafood spots. Views of passing freighters and the just-caught seafood, including hearty Charlie's Chowder, are treats (810/329-2261). For an overnight stay in St. Clair, consider the tony St. Clair Inn, a 1920s Tudor-style water-front inn. Doubles from $90 (800/482-8327).

SIGHTSEEING
Hop aboard the Blue Water Trolley (10 cents) and tour the local sights. You'll pass historic homes from the city's lumbering era, the site of the old Fort Gratiot and the Thomas Edison Depot Historical Site. Fort Gratiot Lighthouse, the oldest light along the Great Lakes, marks the entrance to the St. Clair Straits. Red bricks peek through weathered

white paint on the 80-foot-tall tower, which dates to 1829, about 8 years before Michigan gained statehood. Tour the still-operating light by appointment (800/852-4242).

In nearby Pine Grove Park, visit the 97-foot Huron Lightship Museum (810/982-0891), which dates to the 1920s and is the only remaining vessel of its kind in the state. Lightships were

Three miles of dunes and beaches draw visitors to Port Crescent State Park near Bay City, Michigan.

constructed as floating lighthouses and anchored in areas where permanent lighthouses weren't possible. The Huron is part of The Port Huron Museum, which has an exhibit about Edison's 1850s boyhood home (810/982-0891).

For an even closer look at the lake, sign up for a trip on the Huron Lady, a 65-foot excursion boat that cruises under the Blue Water Bridge and heads out to Lake Huron, where it treats passengers to views of giant freighters loading and unloading cargo. Order a picnic lunch in advance for $5 (888/873-6726).

FISHING

Salmon, perch and bass lure anglers in the spring; Great Lakes trout and walleye attract in summer. A large charter fleet takes anglers of all skill levels onto Lake Huron. The *Miss Port Austin* is a 20-passenger boat available for charters and private parties (517/738-5271). The Thumb Area Charter Captains Association offers regular charter excursions, complete with bait, lures and cleaning afterward (800/35-THUMB).

GOLF

There are more than 15 respected courses in Michigan's Thumb, from beginner to pro levels (800/4GOLF-MI).

ANTIQUES

Michigan's Thumb has some of the state's best antiques malls: Bay City Antiques Center, the state's largest antiques mall (517/893-1116); the 30,000-square-foot Antique Warehouse in Saginaw (517/755-4343); Antiques By-The-Bridge in Sebewaing (517/883-9424).

FESTIVALS

Each summer, thousands of vacationers arrive for the 10-day Blue Water Festival, held in mid-July. The celebration climaxes with the famous Port Huron to Mackinac Island sailboat race, the largest freshwater regatta in the world (800/852-4242).

OTHER PLACES TO VISIT IN THE AREA
Saginaw

One of the most unusual tourist attractions is the Japanese Cultural Center and Tea House in Saginaw. This unique showplace along Lake Linton, designed by Uataro Suzu, was a gift from Saginaw's sister city of Tokushima in Japan. Participate in the ages-old tea service, enjoy a free garden tour or wander through the serene, simple garden (517/759-1648).

Also worth visiting is the free Marshall M. Fredericks Sculpture Gallery at Saginaw Valley State University. The soaring space houses an extraordinary collection of more than 200 works by the world-renowned sculptor best known for his *Spirit of Detroit* work in front of the City-County Building (517/790-5667).

For a truly memorable place to stay, consider Saginaw's Montague Inn. This restored Georgian-style mansion dates to 1929 and welcomes guests in 18 rooms furnished with antiques. Doubles from $75 (517/752-3939).

Frankenmuth

Bavarian atmosphere and legendary chicken dinners draw visitors to Frankenmuth, 20 miles south of Bay City via I-75. The city began as a Sunday drive destination in the 1920s, but has bloomed into the state's largest tourist attraction.

Visitors come for the chicken dinners served at Zehnder's and Bavarian Inn, as well as for shopping at Bronner's, the world's largest Christmas store. Families from across the state head to the Bavarian Inn Lodge, where the Family Fun Center includes three indoor pools (one with a waterfall), miniature golf, games and more.

Nearby Birch Run is home to the state's largest outlet mall, with more than 200 stores boasting brand names. Contact: Frankenmuth Convention & Visitors Bureau, 635 Main St., Frankenmuth, MI 48732 (517/652-6106); Saginaw County Convention & Visitors Bureau, One Tuscola St., Suite 101, Saginaw, MI 48607 (800/444-9979).

By Khristi S. Zimmeth

LAKE ERIE

For 200 true-blue miles, Lake Erie shapes Ohio's northern border. From the brawny port city of Toledo on the west to the tiny towns that hug the Pennsylvania state line on the east, the lake skims along with barely a trace of a cove, inlet or bay—with one grand exception. Midway between Toledo and Cleveland, a fishhook-shaped finger of land curls boldly out into the water. The Marblehead and Catawba peninsulas have defined the Buckeye State's northern vacation country since derbied gentlemen and corsetted ladies toting wicker picnic hampers arrived by steamer to spend a day at the beach.

The lake figured prominently in our country's early history, too. During the War of 1812, Oliver Hazard Perry commanded the small naval fleet of a very young United States of America in the Battle of Lake Erie. He soundly defeated the larger, more experienced British forces and announced his victory with the memorable message "We have met the enemy and they are ours."

You can visit a towering monument to Perry on South Bass Island, one of a cluster of intriguing islands off Catawba and Marblehead. Ride the elevator up to the top of the dramatic 352-foot column for a one-of-a-kind look at the lake, the islands and the shoreline towns.

Those towns include Sandusky, home to Cedar Point Amusement Park, famed the world over for its collection of roller coasters. A dozen of the sinuous, stomach-churning behemoths, from clattery old-fashioned wooden models to sleek space-age newcomers, dot the park.

Head east along the shore and before long you're in

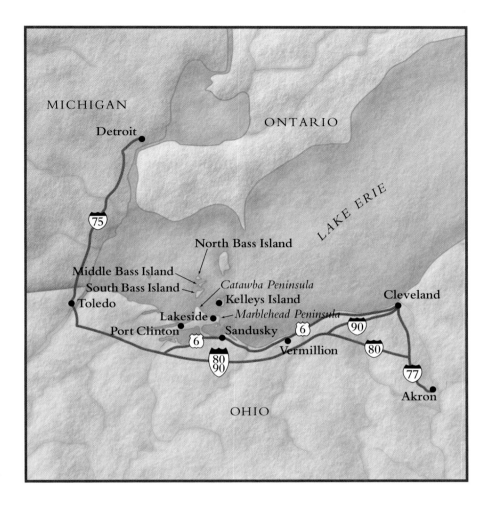

the suburbs of sprawling Cleveland. The city was an industrial giant from the Victorian age through World War II, and John D. Rockefeller was only one millionaire among many who called Cleveland home. Cleveland's legacy from those years is a handsome collection of cultural institutions—museums, theaters, universities, a world-class orchestra—and 19th-century neighborhoods where shops and restaurants are tucked into fanciful old buildings.

Strutting its stuff along a fresh-scrubbed lakefront, Cleveland has built on its past. Among the star attractions are a new baseball stadium, a riverside entertainment district that lights up the night and the Rock and Roll Hall of Fame and Museum.

OHIO'S NORTH COAST

Rollicking amusement parks and serene islands meet in this fun-for-all playground.

Midway along the 115-mile ribbon of Lake Erie shoreline that stretches between Toledo on the west and Cleveland on the east is Ohio's sunny, summertime playground. Surf and sand provide the backdrop for pleasure rides from solitary birdwatching to scream-in-unison roller coasters.

Sandy-shored Marblehead and Catawba peninsulas curve into the water here, pointing north to islands that skip across Lake Erie like stepping stones to fun. To the peninsulas' south, across a boat-filled bay, is the resort town of Sandusky, famed for its dizzying collection of roller coasters. And all along the sun-drenched shorelines of the peninsulas and mainland, Victorian-era villages welcome vacationers as they have for more than a century.

Sandusky

More than 6 million thrill-seekers head to the Sandusky area each year. Most are drawn by the chance to be spun, twisted, dropped or turned upside down at 128-year-old Cedar Point, one of the world's oldest and most popular amusement parks.

With 12 "scream machines," Cedar Point is a mecca for roller-coaster fans. It boasts nearly 50 more down-to-earth rides spread out over 364 acres. Eighteen acres of wet and watery fun, including a 500,000-gallon wave pool, wait at adjacent Soak City Water Park. At Challenge Park, kids can play miniature golf or try piloting sleek race cars.

Carousels may seem a bit tame after Cedar Point's raucous roller coasters, but they have a nostalgic appeal that's always popular. Relive the ride's glory days with a tour of Sandusky's Merry-Go-Round Museum, housed in a historic downtown post office. Then, ride the restored 1930s Allen Herschel carousel—a free spin is included in the tour.

Island Hopping

It's just a short ferryboat ride from Sandusky and the towns of Port Clinton and Marblehead on the peninsula to the simple, old-time pleasures of Lake Erie's islands. Hop aboard for one of the frequent ferry runs to three of the five principal islands.

SANDUSKY/ERIE COUNTY CONVENTION & VISITORS BUREAU

Flags snap to attention in the Lake Erie breeze.

Peaceful Kelleys Island (named for the brothers who bought the island in 1830) is the largest American island on Lake Erie. Listed in the National Register of Historic Places, 2,800-acre Kelleys has been recognized by *Vacations* magazine as one of America's Top Ten Undiscovered Places.

Once on the island, visitors wander the pristine shoreline or travel leafy lanes via bike or golf cart (rentals are available). Popular sites include the Glacial Grooves State Memorial on the island's north side, considered one of the finest glacial markings in the world, and Inscription Rock State Memorial on the island's south side, with ancient prehistoric pictographs of animals and humans by long-ago Native Americans.

Put-in-Bay, the bustling Victorian-era port on nearby South Bass Island, once protected sailors during stormy weather. Now, it's a haven for vacationers looking for sun and fun. Along Main Street, a small antique carousel turns, while shoppers wander in and out of boutiques overflowing with breezy resort fashions and nautical-themed souvenirs.

For a spectacular seagull's-eye view, climb the steps (or take the easy-on-your-feet elevator) 352 feet to the top of Perry's Victory and International Peace Memorial. To get to the bottom of things, join other spelunkers on 20-minute tours beneath the island at Perry's Cave. The monument and cave are named for naval hero Commodore Oliver Perry, who harbored his boats here during the War of 1812. Legend has it that Perry kept prisoners and supplies in the 208-foot cave during the Battle of Lake Erie.

Plan your visit to Middle Bass Island for August and you'll be serenaded by the barbershop quartets gathered for an annual sing-off. While you're here, tour the castlelike buildings of the 19th-century Lonz Winery and marvel at the wine cellars dug by hand during the Civil War. Middle Bass and its

Cedar Point's Ferris wheel lights the night sky.

DENNIS COX

DENNIS COX

**East Quarry Trail
in Kelleys Island
State Park.**

neighbors, North Bass and South Bass, were named for the abundant smallmouth bass found in these cold, clear waters. Bountiful catches have attracted anglers—including Presidents Harrison and Cleveland—for years.

On the Peninsula

Serenity reigns in Lakeside, an idyllic community known as the "Chautauqua on Lake Erie." Families have been coming to this historic Victorian cottage community on the Marblehead Peninsula, east of Port Clinton, since before the late 19th century.

Religious leaders once gathered here for retreat and renewal. As more families joined them, the community's reputation as a vacation paradise spread. Now, visitors spend summer days swimming, sailing, fishing or strolling along the scenic 700-foot dock. Although religious life is still a part of the Lakeside experience, the emphasis today is on fellowship, personal growth and art appreciation. In keeping with its old-time image,

Lakeside also hosts one of the country's most important national shuffleboard tournaments each year.

Day visitors can pick up a pass for activities ranging from the Lakeside Symphony and lectures by visiting scholars to old-fashioned children's programs. To truly experience Lakeside, consider an overnight stay at the grand, 100-room Victorian Hotel Lakeside. From its sprawling front porch, relish panoramic views of Lake Erie and its marvelous sunsets.

Not far from Lakeside is Marblehead, a beacon for lighthouse enthusiasts and home to a small arts community. Tour the oldest operating lighthouse along the Great Lakes, and you'll learn that the light once was fueled by 13 whale-oil lamps and that the limestone lighthouse was built in just 11 weeks. Here, and along the rest of Ohio's north shore, there's a comfortable blending of yesterday's history and today's delights. Best of all, you're never far from the lake's whispering surf and glistening beaches.

Planning Your Visit to Ohio's North Coast

To explore Ohio's Lake Erie shore, head for coastal roads such as State 2, US-6 and US-20. For information, contact: Sandusky/ Erie County Visitors & Convention Bureau (800/255-ERIE) and Ottawa County Visitors Bureau (800/441-1271).

Sandusky and Cedar Point
LODGINGS

The Hotel Breakers— In Cedar Point, it's the oldest place to stay and one-time host to six presidents, Laurel and Hardy, and Annie Oakley. Sandcastle Suites, also part of the park, offers suites and a quiet location away from the park's hubbub. Doubles from $105 (888/775-4242).

Choose from nearly 70 chain hotels outside the park. Comfort Inn-Maingate—It's one block from the causeway with an outdoor pool and a restaurant. Doubles from $58 (800/228-5150). Holiday Inn Express— Doubles from $59 (419/624-0028). Radisson Harbour Inn—An on-site TGI Friday's Restaurant is a great place for a late-night bite. Doubles from $119 (800/333-3333).

DINING

Breakwater Cafe— Situated on the park grounds, it welcomes grown-ups and kids with fresh fish, sandwiches and a stunning sunset view over Lake Erie. Angry Trout Fish and Steakhouse—This family-friendly eatery in nearby Bay View specializes in fresh walleye, trout and perch (419/684-5900).

ACTIVITIES

Cedar Point Amusement Park & Resort—Its 59 rides include 12 roller coasters. An aquarium, Lake Erie beach and live musical shows add to the fun. Soak City Water Park and Challenge Park— They're adjacent to Cedar Point, with miniature golf, race cars and other family attractions. Separate admission prices (419/627-2350). *Red Witch*—This 77-foot classic Alden topsail schooner seats 49 passengers. It's the only boat of its kind plying the Lake Erie waters (419/798-1244). Harbor Bay Golf Dome— Perfect your chip shot or practice putting on a manicured sand-filled green under this 40,000-square-foot air-supported dome in Huron. A PGA professional is available for private lessons or group clinics

(419/433-5549). Sawmill Creek Resort Golf Course—This championship 18-hole course is near the Sawmill Creek Resort in Huron (419/433-3789). Edison Canoe Livery— In Milan, sign on for a 7-mile, 2½-hour trip down the Huron River (419/499-8107). Birdwatching—Lake Erie's diverse shoreline attracts more than 300 bird species. Its vast marshlands harbor herons and egrets. Migratory warblers fill the deep forests. Free bird-watching guides and a list of special events are available (800/255-ERIE). Seneca Caverns—Cave enthusiasts head south of Sandusky to Bellevue. Discovered in 1872, the fascinating caverns have attracted families for more than 50 years (419/483-6711). Historic Lyme Village— It's a re-created 19th-century town in Bellevue (800/562-6978). Sandusky Area Maritime Museum—Explore the city's rich maritime history through artifacts, photos, maps and more (419/624-0274). The Firelands Winery— West of Sandusky along US-6, this award-winning winery offers tastings, tours and a multimedia show. Pick your own grapes during the fall harvest (800/548-WINE).

Lake Erie Islands

Ferries offer frequent service from the mainland. Miller Boat Line provides 18-minute rides to Put-in-Bay and Middle Bass from Catawba Point (800/500-2421). Jet Express serves Put-in-Bay (800/245-1538). Kelleys Island Ferry Boat Lines serves Kelleys with reasonable rates and frequent ferries (419/798-9763). The Emerald Express and the M.V. Goodtime I offer cruises from downtown Sandusky.

Explore the shops and restaurants in Put-in-Bay, the main city on popular South Bass Island.

Kelleys Island

Visit Glacial Grooves State Memorial, one of the largest examples of early glacial activity in the world. Kelleys, with all 2,800 acres, is listed in the National Register of Historic Places. Golf carts and bikes provide easy access to the park and the island's fine beaches. Be sure to see Inscription Rock, a series of pictographs carved by ancient Native Americans. An island park has campsites. Contact: Kelleys Island Chamber of Commerce (419/746-2360).

LODGINGS

Accommodations include: Kelleys Mansion Inn—This historic bed and breakfast has hosted several U.S. presidents. Doubles from $79 (419/746-2273). Craft's Lakeview Lane Motel and Cottages—It's simple, cozy and perfect for those on a budget. Doubles from $60 (419/746-2254). House on Huntington Lane—This lovingly restored home is close to town. Doubles from $75 (419/746-2765). Eagle's Nest—Snug air-conditioned cabins are in a tranquil wooded setting. Doubles from $85 (419/746-2708). Sweet Valley Inn—A horse-drawn buggy carries guests from the ferry dock to an antiques-filled inn. Doubles from $75 (419/746-2750).

DINING

The Village Pump—This local favorite serves lake perch dinners and brandy Alexanders by the pitcherful (419/746-2281).

South Bass Island

South Bass and its main city, Put-in-Bay, is one of the most popular of the Lake Erie Islands. Take a narrated tour with the Island Transportation Tour Train, which stops at Lake Erie battle sites, the towering Perry's Victory and International Peace Memorial and the grounds of the once-grand Victory Hotel (419/285-4855). For more information, contact: Chamber of Commerce (419/285-2832).

LODGINGS

Good bets include: The Ivy Cottages—It's in the woods, away from crowds. Doubles from $125 (419/285-2330). Maple Cottage—This lodging caters to couples only. Doubles from $95 (419-285-4144). Wisteria Inn—This historic home is near the airport. Doubles from $85 (419/285-2828). South Shore Beach Resort—This lakefront site offers condominiums with two bedrooms and two baths from $200 (419/285-4321).

DINING
Pasquale's Cafe on the Village Park—This eatery serves Italian specialties and home-made ice cream (419/285-8600). The Boardwalk—The island's only waterfront restaurant is known for fabulous views and sand-wiches (419/285-3695). Crescent Tavern—This dining spot serves fine food in a Victorian set-ting (419/285-4211).

ACTIVITIES
Bikes and golf carts are available from Island Bike Rental (419/285-2016) and the Park Cart & Bike Rental (419/285-4595), in downtown Put-in-Bay.

Middle Bass Island
Once called the "Island of Flowers," Middle Bass is best known as home of the historic Lonz Winery. The castlelike structure is visible from other islands and accessible by ferryboat (419/285-5411). Middle Bass is one of the least inhabited of the Lake Erie Islands, with two

simple, yet comfortable places to stay: Bass Isle Resort Campground and Cottages—one-bedroom cabins from $55 (800/837-5211) and Johnston's Lakefront Cottages—Cottages, apartments and lodge are available weekly from $285 (800/871-6225).

Lakeside and Marblehead
Pick up a daily pass to enjoy Lakeside's dock, shops and special events. Consider a stay at the 1870s Hotel Lakeside. Its wide front porch

Tony Packo's Cafe on Toledo's east side serves hot dogs with Hungarian hot peppers that pack a punch.

inspires with terrific sunset views. Doubles with shared bath from $25 (419/798-4461). Same Time, Next Year—Family-size suites are available. Doubles from $90 (800/494-5400). For information, contact: Lakeside Association (419/798-4461). Marblehead Lighthouse—Off Bayshore Road in Marblehead is the oldest continuously operating

lighthouse along the Great Lakes. Operated by the U. S. Coast Guard, the light is open for tours the second Saturday of each month from June-October. Richmond Galleries—Art in this downtown Marblehead gallery includes local impressions of the light-house and other landmarks. Margaret Thatcher and Charlton Heston collect the works of owner Ben Richmond (419/798-5631). Prehistoric Forest—Surprise the kids with a walk through a dinosaur-filled forest and a volcano inhabited by prehistoric creatures; it's along State-163 (419/798-5230).

LODGINGS
Old Stone House Bed & Breakfast—Built by a local quarry owner in 1861, this residence welcomes families. Doubles from $75 (419/798-5922).

DINING

Good choices in Marblehead: Crow's Nest is the place for hickory-smoked ribs and Betty's famous salad. Big Boppers has won several chili cook-offs. Frontwaters Restaurant and Brewery serves seafood and pasta specialties, as well as a "brew with a view."

AREA FISHING

Drop a line in Lake Erie, and you'll soon learn why the area's sport-fishing reputation continues to grow. The lake's warm temperatures and shallow reefs provide perfect grounds for walleye, yellow perch, smallmouth bass, catfish, largemouth bass, white bass, crappie and other catches. Whether heading to the lake's western basin and Sandusky Bay or to the deeper waters of the central basin, anglers take home impressive catches. The area is even known as the "Walleye Capital of the World," with a record 15-pound catch by an angler off Sandusky Bay in 1995. Fishing charters include: Captain Hook Charters in Sandusky (800/453-8403) and Shore-Nuf Charters in Port Clinton, with "walk-on" charters from April—October, weather permitting (419/734-9999).

OTHER PLACES TO VISIT IN THE AREA

Vermilion

Follow the lakeshore east to the beautifully preserved coastal town of Vermilion. The Inland Seas Maritime Museum (440/967-3467) displays the nation's leading collection of Great Lakes memorabilia. Wander among rare photographs of shipwrecks and rescued artifacts from sunken ships, even a timber from the Niagara, Commodore Perry's flagship. To experience Lake Erie's majesty firsthand, sign on at McGarvey's Restaurant for an old-fashioned paddle-wheel excursion down the Vermilion River (440/967-8000).

Admire the town square and opera house, then stop at Ednamae's Ice Cream Parlor and Restaurant for delicious, homemade ice cream, as well as soups and sandwiches (440/967-7733). Check out the Old Prague Restaurant, where authentic Czechoslovakian cuisine is served amid an Old World atmosphere (440/967-7182). For more information, contact: Vermilion Chamber of Commerce (440/967-4477).

Toledo

From the Lake Erie Islands, it's a 30-minute drive west to Toledo, Ohio's fourth-largest city. Children will want to see the Center of Science and Industry, known here as COSI. A branch of the well-loved science museum in Columbus, it gives big and little explorers the chance to climb into a space shuttle, ride a bike across a tightrope and experiment with the forces of nature. Preschoolers love climbing into the tree house, "diagnosing" Mom and Dad in the walk-in medical clinic and getting wet at the water table.

The Toledo Museum of Art is famous for its glass collection and paintings by masters such as Monet and Picasso.

At the Toledo Zoo, have lunch in a brightly painted cage in the former lion house.

Don't miss the chance to down a dog at Tony Packo's Cafe, a Hungarian restaurant on the city's east side that was made famous by native son Jamie Farr of M*A*S*H (419/691-6054). For more information, contact: Toledo Convention & Visitors Bureau (800/243-4667).

By Khristi S. Zimmeth

133

CLEVELAND

The metropolis along Lake Erie has reinvented itself. It rocks, it rolls, it's the "Comeback City."

Cleveland threw itself a bicentennial birthday bash in 1996, complete with awe-inspiring fireworks, lively street parties and waterfront frolics. The event marked the city's founding more than 200 years ago by Moses Cleveland, the leader of a plucky band of pioneers who headed westward from Connecticut in 1796.

The bicentennial is past, but the celebration continues. This hardworking town of 505,600 along Lake Erie's southern shore has earned the nickname "Comeback City," polishing its urban image with two bright recent additions to downtown: the dazzling, modern Rock and Roll Hall of Fame and Museum and the endearingly nostalgic baseball stadium, Jacobs Field, home of the Cleveland Indians.

Longtime sites have been smartly updated, too. Visitors crisscross prettily-planted Public Square, the fountain- and monument-studded plaza that has anchored downtown since the city's founding. Dominating the plaza is Tower City Center, a complex of shops and restaurants in a majestic train station, presided over by Cleveland's 42-story Art Deco landmark, Terminal Tower. A short walk up Euclid Avenue is the much-loved Arcade, a three-story Victorian wonder of glass and ironwork enclosing boutiques and eateries.

Along the Lakefront

You may find it hard to keep your toes from tapping while you tour the Rock and Roll Hall of Fame and Museum, which debuted on the city's spiffy North Coast Harbor waterfront in 1995. Designed by world-renowned architect I.M. Pei (mastermind of the expansion of Paris' Louvre Museum), the sparkling $92-million landmark towers like a beacon above the Lake Erie shoreline.

Inside, you'll dance your way through the decades as you tour musical memorabilia ranging from early Elvis to recent rap. More than 50,000 square feet of exhibition space explores rock's ongoing evolution and its impact on American culture. Baby boomers take note: Don't miss John Lennon's psychedelic painted Rolls Royce and Jimi Hendrix's funky patchwork velvet jacket.

Nearby, at the new 165,000-square-foot Great

O.G.S., INC./THE PICTURE CUBE, INC.

Boat passengers on the Cuyahoga River get a closeup look at downtown Cleveland.

Lakes Science Center, explorers of all ages marvel at the more than 350 hands-on exhibits and an awe-inspiring Omnimax theater.

For more waterside fun, you'll want to wander the Flats, the spirited entertainment and restaurant district where the Cuyahoga River meets Lake Erie. Just west of Public Square, this once-grimy industrial area now sparkles, attracting more than 7 million people annually. They come to stroll the riverfront boardwalk, feast in more than 60 restaurants and party until the early morning hours in nightclubs and bars. Nearby is the Historic Warehouse District, where 19th-century store-fronts provide a backdrop for a neighborhood of cafes, art galleries and nightclubs featuring live jazz and blues.

Cultural Cleveland

Despite the city's industrial bent, Cleveland has never overlooked the finer things in life. The century-old Cleveland Orchestra is recognized as one of America's finest, and its lovely performance space, Severance Hall, has been judged acoustically perfect. The Cleveland Museum of Art displays paintings, sculpture and precious objects from around the globe amassed by the industrialists who built the city's

fortunes. Free Wednesday night performances draw crowds to the lively, internationally respected Cleveland Institute of Music. All three institutions are located in University Circle, a concentration of arts and educational institutions in a parklike setting just 4 miles east of downtown. University Circle also is home to the Cleveland Play House, the oldest regional theater in the country, and the Karamu House, the nation's oldest multicultural center for the arts.

The city long has been known for its theaters. Downtown, Playhouse Square Center is made up of four splendid theaters that have been restored: the Ohio, State, Palace and Allen. The second-largest arts center in America, this lively complex hosts glamorous Broadway-style musicals, the Cleveland Opera, the Cleveland Ballet and other lavish stage productions. Nearby, the newly renovated Hanna Theatre features cabaret entertainment.

Kid-Friendly Places

If you're exploring University Circle's diverse riches with youngsters along, the Cleveland Museum of Natural History, Ohio's largest natural sciences museum, is a must—don't miss the dinosaurs! Stop by the Western

Cleveland Indians fans at Jacobs Field.

COURTESY OF THE CLEVELAND INDIANS/GREGORY DREZDON

BRUCE ZAKE

The Arcade decked out for Christmas.

Reserve Historical Society's meticulously restored 1911 Hay–McKinney mansion, for a peek at the past. The society's Crawford Auto-Aviation Museum houses more than 200 classic automobiles and aircraft.

One of the most unusual of the city's museums is the Health Museum, where more than 200 exhibits—including the world's largest tooth and Juno, a transparent talking woman—encourage good health and make up the first museum of its kind in the nation. Another can't-miss attraction (especially if you have any would-be astronauts in tow) is the NASA Lewis Research Center, the only NASA facility north of the Mason-Dixon line and a leading research base for aerospace technology. Highlights include a space shuttle, space station, an Apollo capsule and Skylab 3.

Cleveland's Great Outdoors

Encircling the city is one of the nation's largest metropolitan parks systems, the 100-mile long, 14-location Cleveland Metroparks. From the air, the more than 19,000 acres that make up the park system resemble an emerald necklace in richness and color. Outdoor lovers can hike, bike, canter on horseback along bridle trails or stroll through acres of lush landscape. Popular with plant lovers is the Cleveland Botanical Garden. More than 7 acres display theme gardens ranging from All-America roses to serene Japanese settings.

Cleveland's foresighted visionaries saw the need to preserve Lake Erie for recreation, as well as for industry. One result is Cleveland Lakefront State Park. This popular park has miles of paved bike paths, nature walks and fitness trails, along with fishing piers, picnic areas and sandy beaches where kids of all ages can build sandcastles or play tag with the surf.

Anglers aren't forgotten. Some 400,000 registered boaters take to the lake's deep blue-green waters annually, enjoying, some say, the best walleye fishing in the world.

Those who prefer to relax and leave the navigating to someone else can opt for a romantic evening cruise along the Cuyahoga River and the Lake Erie shore. As you glide through the quiet waters, you'll see the city's majestic bridges lit in rainbow colors, a lasting legacy of the bicentennial and a glowing salute to Ohio's "Comeback City."

Planning Your Visit to Cleveland

For information, contact: Convention & Visitors Bureau of Greater Cleveland (800/321-1001). For area information, contact: Ohio Division of Travel & Tourism (800/BUCKEYE).

LODGINGS

Several downtown hotels are within walking distance of shops and theaters. Good choices include: The 208-room Ritz-Carlton Cleveland, with china cabinets in the halls and fine art on the walls. Doubles from $169 (216/623-1300; 800/241-3333). Renaissance Cleveland Hotel is an elegant 491-room vintage hotel recognized by Historic Hotels of America. Doubles from $135 (800/468-3571). Sheraton Cleveland City Center has 475 rooms, many with lake views. Doubles from $139 (800/321-1090). A new option in the theater district is the Wyndham Cleveland, named by *Cleveland* magazine as the place where visitors are "Most Likely to See Stars" because of its proximity to the theater district. For a real treat, ask for one of the corner rooms. Doubles from $129 (216/615-7500). Away from downtown, try the Baricelli Inn in the Little Italy area. The three-story 1900 brownstone's seven rooms are decorated with antiques and stained glass. Doubles from $125 (216/791-6500).

RESTAURANTS

Otto Moser's in the Playhouse Square district is a local institution, a casual eatery where diners line up for the chance to sample the German potato salad and other house specials. Walls are lined with auto-graphed portraits of stars (216/771-3831). For a special-occasion splurge, enjoy memorable meals at the prestigious four-diamond Classics Restaurant in the Omni International Hotel near University Circle (216/791-1300); the Mediterranean-flavored Sans Souci in the Renaissance Cleveland Hotel (216/696-5600); and the Ritz Carlton's Riverview Room (216/623-1300).

In the Flats, head to the riverfront Watermark for marinated and grilled seafood and great views of the Cuyahoga (216/241-1600). Nearby is the more casual, but no less popular, Shooters on the Water (216/861-6900) and Landry's (216/566-1010), both good places for salads and sandwiches.

Near West Side Market, the Great Lakes Brewing Company lures diners with a historic 1860s brewery atmosphere and a menu of crab cakes, fresh pastas and the house special, the brew master's pie (216/771-4404).

For traditional Italian food, go to the city's oldest restaurant, Guarino's, near University Circle in the area known as Little Italy (216/231-3100).

For Chinese cuisine, Szechwan Garden in Lakewood is among the best in the city, with a variety of mild and hot entrées, including the house special, "Happy Family" with shrimp, chicken and beef (216/226-1987).

Other favorites: Parker's in the revital-ized Ohio City neighbor-hood about a 5-minute ride from downtown. The food is hearty and French-style, with changing entrées of lamb, seafood, beef and poultry served nightly during five-course prix-fixe menus (216/771-7130).

Kids will like the Spaghetti Warehouse, where you can dine inside a trolley car on a wide variety of pastas

(216/621-9420).

Discover more Mediterranean cuisine at the New York Spaghetti House, where murals of Italy line the walls of a former parsonage. Homemade pastas and veal are the house specialties (216/696-6624).

For a truly tasty experience, consider a

Tasty treats await in the small shops and restaurants of the Little Italy neighborhood near University Circle.

visit to the city's classic West Side Market at West 25th Street and Lorain Avenue. Here, the city's many ethnic groups meet to buy and sell fresh fruit, vegetables, meats, fish, poultry, cheese and more. Wander among the stalls and pick from just-baked goodies or a freshly made sandwich to enjoy alfresco. Call for information about

opening and closing times (216/664-3386).

TOURS

"Lolly the Trolley" offers 1- and 2-hour sightseeing tours that are a good introduction to the city (216/771-4484). For a wonderful view, head for the 42nd floor of Cleveland's Terminal Tower (216/621-7981).

To see Cleveland's waterfront areas from a new vantage point, board the four-decked 1,000-passenger Goodtime III for a daytime or evening sail along the Cuyahoga River and Lake Erie (216/861-5110). Sign up for a gourmet dinner cruise on the elegant, 300-passenger Nautica Queen (216/696-8888).

A free "Cleveland

Card" with more than $500 in savings at area restaurants, hotels, shops and sightseeing spots is available from the Convention & Visitors Bureau of Greater Cleveland.

MUSEUMS

Museums mentioned in the main story: Rock and Roll Hall of Fame and Museum (One Key Plaza, 216/781-ROCK); Great Lakes Science Center (North Coast Harbor, 216/694-2000); Cleveland Museum of Art (11150 East Blvd., 216/421-7340); Cleveland Museum of Natural History (One Wade Oval Dr., 216/231-4600); Health Museum of Cleveland (8911 Euclid Ave., 216/231-5010); Western Reserve Historical Society (216/721-5722); NASA Lewis Research Center (216/433-4000).

Nautical nuts and military buffs will enjoy touring the Steamship William G. Mather Museum, a floating maritime collection in a restored 1925 Great Lakes freighter (216/574-6262) and the USS Cod, a World War II fleet submarine that remains unaltered. Navy submarine veterans act as tour guides, giving visitors a real sense of life on board (216/566-8770).

TRAVEL GUIDE

SHOPPING

Downtown, don't miss the $400-million Avenue at Tower City Center, a grand old train depot turned shopping mecca with an 80-foot skylight and a whopping 26 elevators. Enter through Terminal Tower on Public Square to shop at Liz Claiborne, J. Crew, Ann Taylor and others (216/623-4750). The glass-enclosed Galleria at Erieview houses 60 shops, including Eddie Bauer and the Cleveland Indians Gift Shop (216/861-4343). Walk in the footsteps of generations of Clevelanders who have browsed the boutiques of the multistoried Arcade on Euclid Ave. It's a 19th-century crystal palace (216/621-8500).

Those looking for vintage treasures can head to Lorain Avenue. The area from W. 25th to W. 117th streets, and Detroit to Westwood Avenues is known as "Antique Row." More antiques shops are in the westside Ohio City neighborhood. Country furniture and collectible china crowd the dozen-plus shops that dot the appealing Shaker Square area (216/751-9204).

Outlet shoppers can bag a bargain or two at the Aurora Premium Factory Outlets near Sea World and Geauga Lake (330/562-2000).

SPORTS

Cleveland boasts enviable big-league action year-round. Gateway Sports Entertainment Complex opened in 1994 and includes Jacobs Field, noted for the largest scoreboard in the U.S. The complex is home to the Cleveland Indians, as well as Gund Arena, host of Cleveland Cavaliers basketball, Cleveland Lumberjacks hockey and more than

Ramón Thielen and Nancy Latoszewski of the Cleveland Ballet, one of the city's outstanding cultural assets.

BRUCE ZAKE

200 other family events and concerts annually (216/420-2000).

THEATER

Performance spaces mentioned in the main story include:

Playhouse Square Center (216/771-4444); Hanna Theatre (216/771-1664); Cleveland Play House (216/795-7000); Karamu House (216/795-7070); Severance Hall (216/231-7300); and The Cleveland Institute of Music (216/791-5000). For a free map and guide to the University Circle area, call: 216/791-3900.

FLORA AND FAUNA

Cleveland's Metroparks Zoo has more than 3,300 animals from all continents found in more than 165 rolling wooded acres. It's just 5 minutes from downtown. While there, don't miss the Rain Forest exhibit, which features 600 species of animals and 10,000 varieties of plants, trees and shrubs in an elaborate 2-acre bilevel re-creation of a tropical habitat. There is even a 25-foot waterfall and a simulated thunder-storm (216/351-6300).

You'll find more green acres just east of Cleveland in Kirtland, where the Holden Arboretum is known as northeast Ohio's living museum. Here, amateur botanists and other green thumbers can wander among more than 3,000 acres of natural woodlands and the rare horticultural collections (440/946-4400).

GOLF

The Cleveland area boasts seven fine golf courses, from Glenmoor Country Club, a Jack Nicklaus signature course (330/966-3600), to the Tanglewood Country Club, covering more than 7,000 yards of rolling fairways. Tanglewood holds the highest USGA slope rating in northern Ohio (440/543-7010).

NIGHTLIFE

The city's nightlife, like its personality, is eclectic, with something for everyone after dark. The hub is the Flats, once the site of such blockbuster industries as John D. Rockefeller's first oil refinery. Today, converted warehouses house more than 60 restaurants and nightclubs. Live music here ranges from jazz and rock to R&B and reggae. The Nautica Complex, on the west bank, features shopping, dining, a half-mile boardwalk along the river and the Nautica Stage, an open-air, 4,000-seat water-front music pavilion. The Powerhouse, once the headquarters of the city's electric railway, boasts four levels of dining and entertainment. Other recommendations include: Peabody's in the Flats for rock and roll; Darby O'Toole's in North Olmstead for Irish music; Swingo's at the Silver Quill for nostalgic tunes from the 1950s and '60s; and in the Ritz-Carlton Hotel in Tower City Center, classical harp and piano, soothing accompani-ment to a nightcap.

SPECIAL EVENTS

Highlights from the city's calendar of events include: the International Film Festival in March; the Tri-C JazzFest in April; the Great American Rib Cook-Off in June; the Festival of Freedom in July; and the Cleveland National Air Show in September. For details, call: 800/321-1004.

OTHER PLACES TO VISIT IN THE AREA

Chagrin Falls—A short drive east of Cleveland, this picturesque New England-style village is near roaring waterfalls. Boutiques with books, toys, designer-style clothing and unusual home furnishings line the quaint downtown streets. Be sure to stop at the Popcorn Shop for some caramel corn, a local favorite. Head to River Street to find the cluster of renovated cottages that house The Inn of Chagrin Falls. Opt for an over-night stay, a meal at cozy Gamekeepers or leisurely search through country-style clothing and home accessories at Hearthside (216/247-1200). Contact: Chagrin Valley Chamber of Commerce (440/247-6607).

Amish Country—One of the largest Amish communities in the world is less than an hour south of Cleveland, just outside Akron. Visitors enjoy homemade meals, cheese-making demonstrations and shops selling furniture, baskets and quilts of exceptional craftsmanship (800-BUCKEYE).

By Khristi S. Zimmeth

The Grand Hotel, Mackinac Island, page 108.

Indiana Dunes State Park, page 64.

Midwest Living® Books
An imprint of Meredith® Books

Great Lakes Getaways
Project Editor: Judith P. Knuth
Art Director: Angie Hoogensen
Copy Chief: Catherine Hamrick
Copy and Production Editor:
  Terri Fredrickson
Contributing Copy Editor:
  Angela K. Renkoski
Contributing Researchers:
  Joan Luckett, Nancy Singh
Contributing Proofreader:
  Deb Morris Smith
Map Illustrator: Mike Burns
Electronic Production Coordinator:
  Paula Forest
Editorial and Design Assistants:
  Judy Bailey, Kaye Chabot,
  Karen Schirm
Production Director:
  Douglas M. Johnston
Production Manager: Pam Kvitne
Assistant Prepress Manager:
  Marjorie J. Schenkelberg

Meredith® Books
Editor in Chief: James D. Blume
Design Director: Matt Strelecki
Managing Editor: Gregory H. Kayko

Director, Sales & Marketing, Retail:
  Michael A. Peterson
Director, Sales & Marketing, Special
  Markets: Rita McMullen
Director, Sales & Marketing, Home &
  Garden Center Channel: Ray Wolf
Director, Operations: George A. Susral

Vice President, General Manager:
  Jamie L. Martin

Midwest Living® **Magazine**
Editor: Dan Kaercher
Managing Editor: Barbara Humeston

Meredith Publishing Group
President, Publishing Group:
  Christopher M. Little
Vice President, Consumer Marketing
  & Development: Hal Oringer

Meredith Corporation
Chairman and Chief Executive
  Officer: William T. Kerr

Chairman of the Executive
  Committee: E. T. Meredith III

All of us at Meredith® Books are dedicated to providing you with the information and ideas you need. We welcome your comments and suggestions. Write to us at: Meredith® Books, Travel Department, 1716 Locust St., Des Moines, IA 50309-3023.

If you would like to order additional copies of any of our books, check with your local bookstore.

Copyright © 1998 by Meredith
  Corporation, Des Moines, Iowa.
All rights reserved. Printed in the
  United States of America.
First Edition. Printing Number and
  Year: 5 4 3 2 1   02 01 00 99 98
Library of Congress Catalog Card
  Number: 97-76215
ISBN: 0-696-20788-5